Chaucer

THE
Pardoner's
PROLOGUE AND TALE

Edited by David Kirkham and Valerie Allen

CAMBRIDGE
UNIVERSITY PRESS

The publishers would like to thank Professor Helen Cooper for her help in the preparation of this edition.

CAMBRIDGE UNIVERSITY PRESS
Cambridge, New York, Melbourne, Madrid, Cape Town, Singapore, São Paulo, Delhi

Cambridge University Press
The Edinburgh Building, Cambridge CB2 8RU, UK

www.cambridge.org
Information on this title: www.cambridge.org/9780521666459

First published 2000
8th printing 2008

Printed in the United Kingdom at the University Press, Cambridge

A catalogue record for this publication is available from the British Library

ISBN 978-0-521-66645-9 paperback

Prepared for publication by Elizabeth Paren
Designed and formatted by Geoffrey Wadsley
Illustrated by Dave Bowyer
Picture research by Valerie Mulcahy

Thanks are due to the following for permission to reproduce photographs:
Ancient Art and Architecture Collection, page 24; The Bridgeman Art Library, London, pages 15 (Private
Collection), 20 (Public Record Office, London), 38 (British Library, London), 60 (Ashmolean Museum,
Oxford); E.T. Archive/British Library, London, page 67; Mary Evans Picture Library, pages 32, 51, 73; The
Fotomas Index, page 54; Hulton Getty Collection, pages 7, 70, 75; Magnum Photos/Jean Gaumy, page 68

For cover photograph: Canterbury Tales: The Pardoner's Tale, *Ellesmere Manuscript (Facsimile Edition 1911)*,
Private Collection/The Bridgeman Art Library, London

Contents

Introduction   5

What are The Canterbury Tales?   6

Chaucer's language   8

The Pardoner's contribution   11

Text and notes

THE PORTRAIT OF THE PARDONER   12
(from The General Prologue)

INTRODUCTION TO THE PARDONER'S TALE   16

THE PARDONER'S PROLOGUE   20

THE PARDONER'S TALE   30

The tale told by the Pardoner   66

Chaucer's pilgrims   67

Pilgrims and pilgrimages   69

Geoffrey Chaucer   71

Background to the Pardoner's Tale   73

Chaucer's self-examination as a poet   77

The role of the church   78

Themes in the Pardoner's Prologue and Tale   80

Glossary of frequently-used words   80

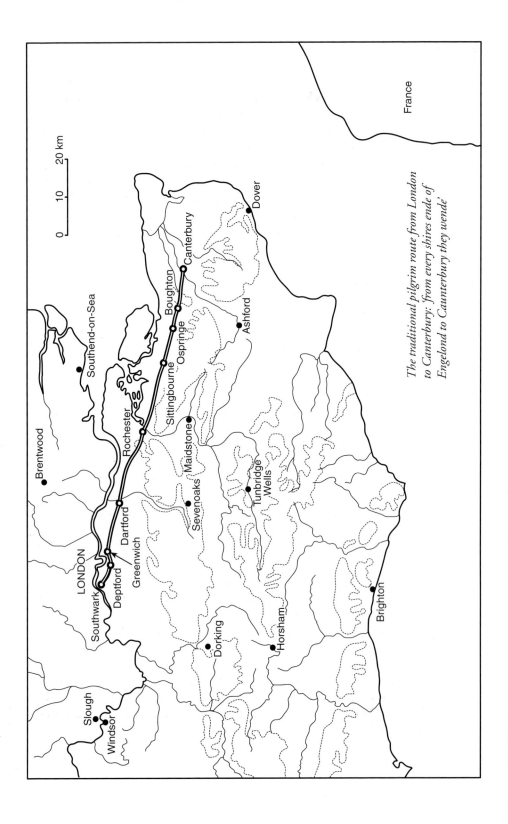

The traditional pilgrim route from London to Canterbury: from every shires ende of Engelond to Caunterbury they wende'

France

Dover

Canterbury
Boughton
Ospringe
Sittingbourne
Ashford
Rochester

Southend-on-Sea

Brentwood

Maidstone

Sevenoaks

Tunbridge Wells

Dartford
Greenwich
LONDON
Deptford
Southwark

Brighton

Horsham

Dorking

Slough
Windsor

0   10   20 km

Introduction

The first encounter with a page of Chaucer in its original form can be a disconcerting experience. Initially, few words look familiar. Even when the meaning has been puzzled out, the reader is faced with an account of people who lived and died in a world very different from our own. The fourteenth century seems very far away, and you might be forgiven for thinking that *The Canterbury Tales* are 'too difficult'.

The aim of this series is, therefore, to introduce you to the world of Chaucer in a way that will make medieval language and life as accessible as possible. With this in mind, we have adopted a layout in which each right-hand page of text is headed by a brief summary of content, and faced by a left-hand page offering a glossary of more difficult words and phrases, as well as commentary notes dealing with style, characterisation and other relevant information. There are illustrations, and suggestions for ways in which you might become involved in the text to help make it come alive.

If initial hurdles are lowered in this way, Chaucer's wit and irony, his ability to suggest character and caricature, and his delight in raising provocative and challenging issues from various standpoints, can more readily be appreciated and enjoyed. There is something peculiarly delightful in discovering that someone who lived six hundred years ago had a sense of humour and a grasp of personalities and relationships as fresh and relevant today as it was then.

Each tale provides considerable material for fruitful discussion of fourteenth century attitudes and modern parallels. It is important to realise that the views expressed by the teller of any one tale are not necessarily Chaucer's own. Many of the activities suggested are intended to make you aware of the multiplicity of voices and attitudes in the *The Canterbury Tales*. A considerable part of the enjoyment comes from awareness of the tongue-in-cheek presence of the author, who allows his characters to speak for themselves, thereby revealing their weaknesses and obsessions.

Essential information contained in each book includes a brief explanation of what *The Canterbury Tales* are, followed by some hints on handling the language. There is then a brief introduction to the teller of the relevant story, his or her portrait from the General Prologue, and an initial investigation into the techniques Chaucer uses to present characters.

The left-hand page commentaries give information applicable to the text. Finally, each book offers a full list of pilgrims, further information on Chaucer's own life and works, some background history, and greater discussion of specific medieval issues. Suggestions for essays and themes to be explored are also included. On page 80 there is a relatively short glossary of words most frequently encountered in the text, to supplement the more detailed glossary on each page.

Chaucer's tales are witty, clever and approachable, and raise interesting parallels with life today. His manipulation of the short story form is masterly. We hope this edition will bring *The Canterbury Tales* alive and allows you to appreciate Chaucer's art with ease and enjoyment.

What are The Canterbury Tales?

They are a collection of stories, loosely linked together, apparently told by a variety of storytellers with very different characters and from different social classes. In fact, both the storytellers themselves and the tales are the creation of one man, Geoffrey Chaucer. Chaucer imagines a group of pilgrims, setting off from the Tabard Inn one spring day on the long journey from London to the shrine of St Thomas à Becket in Canterbury – a journey that on horseback would take about four days.

To make time pass more pleasantly they agree to tell stories to one another. Chaucer begins by introducing his pilgrims to the reader, in descriptions which do much to reveal the characters, vices and virtues of each individual. We learn more from the way each person introduces his or her tale, still more from the tales themselves and the way in which each one is told, and even further information is offered by the manner in which some pilgrims react to what others have to say. By this means Chaucer provides a witty, penetrating insight into the attitudes, weaknesses, virtues and preoccupations of English men and women of the fourteenth century. Some of their behaviour and interests may seem very strange to modern readers; at other times they seem just like us.

THE TALES

Although Chaucer never completed *The Canterbury Tales*, enough of it was completed for us to appreciate the richness of texture and ironical comment Chaucer wove into his tapestry of fourteenth century life. The tales themselves are quite simple – medieval audiences did not expect original plots, but rather clever or unexpected ways of telling stories that might already be known in another form. Chaucer's audiences of educated friends, witty and urbane courtiers, perhaps the highest aristocracy, and even the king and queen, were clearly able to appreciate his skills to the full. Story telling was a leisurely process, since reading was a social rather than a private activity. Since many people could not read, Chaucer would expect the tales to be read aloud. You could try to read them like this – you will find advice on pronunciation on page 9 – and you will discover they become still more lively and dramatic when spoken rather than just read on the page.

Most of the tales in the collection include aspects of at least one of the following categories of tales familiar to Chaucer's audience.

Courtly romances These stories of courtly love affairs were for the upper classes. They often told of unrequited love from a distance, the male lover suffering sleepless nights of anguish, pining away, writing poetry, serenading his beloved with love songs and performing brave feats of noble daring. Meanwhile the beloved (but untouchable) lady would sit in her bower and sew, walk in her castle gardens, set her lover impossible tasks to accomplish, and give him a scarf or a handkerchief as a keepsake.

Fabliaux Extended jokes or tricks, often bawdy, and usually full of sexual innuendo.

Fables These are tales that make a moral point, often using animals as characters.

The destination of the pilgrims – Canterbury Cathedral today

Sermons Sermons were stories with a moral message. Since 95 per cent of society could not read, sermons had to be good, interesting and full of dramatic storytelling. The line between a good story and a good sermon was very thin indeed. Usually there was an abstract theme (gluttony, avarice, pride) and much use was made of biblical and classical parallels or *exempla* to underline the preacher's point.

Confessions The storytellers often look back over their own lives, revealing faults and unhappinesses to the audience. This aspect is usually introduced in the teller's prologue to the actual story.

The tales vary widely in content and tone, since medieval stories, Chaucer's included, were supposed both to instruct and to entertain. Many have an underlying moral; some, such as the Pardoner's Tale, are highly dramatic, and others, like those told by the Knight and the Squire, have their origins firmly in the courtly love tradition. Many are more complex than this suggests. They also vary greatly: Chaucer includes stories as sentimental as that of the Prioress, and as crude and bawdy as those of the Miller and the Reeve.

The device of using different characters to tell different tales allows Chaucer to distance himself from what is being said, and to disguise the fact that he controls the varied and opinionated voices of his creations. He can pretend, for instance, to have no way of preventing the drunken Miller from telling his vulgar story about the carpenter's wife, and he can absolve himself from blame when the tellers become sexually explicit. A modern audience may find his frankness and openness about sex surprising, but it was understandable, for there was little privacy, even for the well-to-do, and sexual matters were no secret. The coarse satire of the fabliaux was as much enjoyed by Chaucer's 'gentil' audience as the more restrained romances.

Chaucer's language

The unfamiliar appearance of a page of Chaucerian English often prevents students from pursuing their investigations any further. It does no good telling them that this man used language with a complexity and subtlety not found in any writer of English anywhere before him. They remain unimpressed. He looks incomprehensible.

In fact, with a little help, it does not take very long to master Chaucer's language. Much of the vocabulary is the same, or at least very similar to, words we use today. On page 80 there is a glossary of the unfamiliar words most frequently used in this text, and these will quickly become familiar. Other words and phrases that could cause difficulties are explained on the page facing the actual text.

The language of Chaucer is known as Middle English – a term covering English as it was written and spoken in the period roughly between 1150 and 1500. It is difficult to be more precise than this, for Middle English itself was changing and developing throughout that period towards 'modern' English.

Old English (Anglo-Saxon) was spoken and written until around 1066, the time of the Norman Conquest. This event put power and authority in England into the hands of the Norman lords, who spoke their own brand of Norman French. Inevitably this became the language of the upper classes. The effect was felt in the church, for speedily the control of the monasteries and nunneries was given to members of the new French-speaking aristocracy. Since these religious houses were the seats of learning and centres of literacy, the effect on language was considerable. If you were a wealthy Anglo-Saxon, eager to get on in the world of your new over-lords, you learnt French. Many people were bi- or even trilingual: French was the language of the law courts and much international commerce; Latin was the language of learning (from elementary learning to the highest levels of scholarship) and the church (from parish church services to the great international institution of the papacy).

Gradually, as inter-marriage between Norman French and English families became more common, the distinction between the two groups and the two languages became blurred. Many French words became absorbed into Old English, making it more like the language we speak today. In the thirteenth century King John lost control of his Norman lands, and as hostility between England and France grew, a sense of English nationalism strengthened. In 1362 the English language was used for the first time in an English parliament. At the same time, Geoffrey Chaucer, a young ex-prisoner of war, was sharpening his pens and his wit, testing the potential for amusement, satire and beauty in this rich, infinitely variable, complex literary tool.

Although some tales are partly, or entirely, in prose, *The Canterbury Tales* are written largely in rhyming iambic couplets. This form of regular metre and rhyme is flexible enough to allow Chaucer to write in a range of styles. He uses the couplet form to imitate colloquial speech as easily as philosophical debate. Most importantly, Chaucer wrote poetry 'for the ear'; it is written for the listener, as much as for the reader. Rhyme and alliteration add emphasis and link ideas and objects together in a way that is satisfying for the audience. The words jog along as easily and comfortably as the imaginary pilgrims and their horses jogged to Canterbury.

PRONUNCIATION

Chaucer spoke the language of London, of the king's court, but he was well aware of differences in dialect and vocabulary in other parts of the country. In the Reeve's Tale, for instance, he mocks the north country accents of the two students. It is clear, therefore, that there were differences in pronunciation in the fourteenth century, just as there are today.

Having been told that Chaucer wrote verse to be read aloud, students may be dismayed to find that they do not know how it should sound. There are two encouraging things to bear in mind. The first is that although scholars feel fairly sure they know something about how Middle English sounded, they cannot be certain, and a number of different readings can still be heard, so no individual performance can be definitely 'wrong'. The second concerns the strong metrical and rhyming structure Chaucer employed in the writing of his tales.

Finding the rhythm Follow the rhythm of the verse (iambic pentameter), sounding or omitting the final 'e' syllable in the word as seems most appropriate. In the line:

> **So dronke he was, he nyste what he wroghte.**

it would add an unnecessary syllable if the final 'e' in 'dronke' and 'wroghte' were to be pronounced. An 'e' at the end of a word almost always disappears if it is followed by a word beginning with 'h' or a vowel.

In the case of these examples:

> **No lenger thanne after Deeth they soughte,**

and

> **That oon of hem the cut broghte in his fest**

the best swing to the regular ten-syllabled line is achieved by sounding the 'e' (as a neutral vowel sound, like the 'u' in put, or the 'a' in about) in the words 'thanne', but not in 'soughte' or 'broghte'.

Other points In words beginning with the letter 'y' (for example 'ywet', 'yknowe') the 'y' is sounded as it would be in the modern 'party'. Many consonants now silent were pronounced – as in 'knight', 'wrong'. All the consonants would be given voice in words such as 'draughtes' and 'knight' and the 'gh' would be sounded like the Scots 'ch' in 'loch'. The combination 'ow' (for example 'yow', meaning 'you') is pronounced as 'how', and the 'ei' in 'streit' would be like the 'a' sound in 'pay'.

For more ideas of what the language might have sounded like, listen to the tapes of Chaucer published by Cambridge University Press and by the 'Chaucer Man' (Trevor Eaton).

WARM-UP ACTIVITIES

- Choose a long, self-contained section from the text: lines 49–79 of the Pardoner's Prologue are a useful example. After a brief explanation of the content, if considered necessary, students work in pairs, speaking alternately, and changing over at each punctuation point. It should be possible to develop a fair turn of speed without losing the sense of the passage.

- Again in pairs, choose about ten lines of text; as one of the pair maintains a steady beat [^/^/^/^/^/] the partner does his or her best to fit the words to the rhythm.
- Choose a long self-contained unit from the text. Students walk round the room, speaking the script, and turning left or right at each punctuation mark. An alternative to this might be to use one 'speaker' to four or five 'listeners', representing Chaucer's audience. Each time the speaker reaches a punctuation mark he/she should switch to a new member of the audience, who should respond by looking alert and animated, being only allowed to sink back into apathy when he/she moves to the next one.

GRAMMATICAL POINTS

Emphatic negatives Whereas a person who stated that 'he wasn't going nowhere, not never' might be considered grammatically incorrect nowadays, Chaucer used double or triple negatives quite often, to give a statement powerful added emphasis. One of the best known is in his description of the Knight in the General Prologue:

> He never yet no vilenye sayde
> In al his life, unto no manner wight.

Another occurs in the Pardoner's Tale:

> Ne I wol nat take on me so greet defame,
> You for to allie unto none hasardours.

In both cases the repeated negative strengthens the force of what is being said.

Word elision In modern written English words and phrases are often run together (elided) to represent the spoken form of these words – 'didn't', 'can't', 'won't', 'I've', and so on. Chaucer uses short forms of words too, especially in forming the negative. In his time it was usual to form a negative by placing 'ne' before the verb. With common verbs this was often elided into the verb. Thus 'ne was' is the Chaucerian form of 'was not', but it was often written as 'nas'. As was seen above, Chaucer writes 'nyste', short for 'ne wyste', meaning 'did not know'.

The 'y' prefix The past participle of a verb sometimes has a 'y' before the rest of the verb, particularly when the verb is passive:

This tresor moste ycaried be	This treasure must be carried
Shal been his sauce ymaked	His sauce shall be made

The 'possessive' form of nouns In modern English we indicate possession by means of an apostrophe: 'the hat of the man' becomes 'the man's hat'. Middle English had a particular formation that is still used in modern German. Where we now use an apostrophe followed by an 's', Chaucer uses the suffix 'es'. So 'the man's hat' becomes 'the mannes hat', the extra 'n' indicating that the word has two syllables.

The Pardoner's contribution

Chaucer promises at the beginning of *The Canterbury Tales* that he will describe all his pilgrims, their status and their personality. He lists them in rough order of precedence, beginning with the Knight and his party, followed by a group of religious characters who have status and importance (the Prioress, the Monk and the Friar), and then down through the social ranks, with well-to-do middle class individuals followed by more lowly commoners. He ends his list with two unashamedly corrupt servants of the church, the Summoner and the Pardoner. A list of the pilgrims who feature in the complete work may be found on page 67.

The Pardoner appears right at the end of the list, a man who declares his contempt for others and his desire for gain with no sign of embarrassment, let alone guilt. He dresses oddly, in a manner entirely unsuited to his rank and function; he is sexually ambiguous and physically repulsive. At the same time he is described as able to affect people with his eloquence and with his impressive bearing in church.

Chaucer gives this character sketch straightforwardly; the listeners have to draw their own conclusions about him, and different members of the party would no doubt draw different conclusions.

The Pardoner's contribution is as individual as he is. It opens with the Host, deeply affected by the fate of the innocent maid in the Doctor's Tale, and trying very hard to ingratiate himself with the Doctor. He then instructs the Pardoner to tell his tale, and to make it a respectable one. His professional eye has perhaps told him that the Pardoner is capable of unashamed smut. The Pardoner asserts his personality immediately – he is not at all put out by this hint of the Host's opinion of him, and he demands time for a drink while he thinks of something suitable.

When it comes, his story is largely of himself. As his Prologue unfolds we learn all about his professional methods as he arrives in some parish to cheat the parishioners out of their tiny savings as they buy his pardons and his relics. Ironically this declaration is followed by 'a moral tale' of the price to be paid for debauchery, gluttony, avarice and murder. He follows the instruction of the Host, though very much in his own way, as he includes his own sermon in the tale. We feel the power of this unorthodox preaching as he blasts the sins arising from gluttony. Abruptly the story returns to the actions and fate of the three young men who seek death and find it. Then, just as abruptly, he returns to his sales pitch trying to sell relics and pardons to the pilgrims. The Host makes his fury clear and delivers a blistering response that makes the Pardoner retreat into silence and anger. The Knight intervenes to bring about a form of reconciliation between the two before the remaining tales can be told.

Paradoxically, the Pardoner, a deeply sinful man with entirely selfish motives, is an effective preacher against sin. He should not be preaching - that was the prerogative of a priest – but he is an impressive churchman and his false relics reflected and encouraged real devotion. His story is more complicated than even he perhaps realises.

The portrait of the Pardoner follows that of the Summoner, an official whose job was to summon people to the church courts. This Summoner is a corrupt man, exploiting people's fears of his powers for gain. The Pardoner is also corrupt, and lives by selling pardons, one of the most bitterly criticised religious practices in the fourteenth century. By buying a pardon you could build up a kind of spiritual bank balance against your sins, provided you also confessed them to a priest and were absolved. The Pardoner also sells 'relics' of saints – pieces of their bones or clothing, etc.

- What impression of the Pardoner's appearance and character do you receive from this introduction? Work out with a partner exactly how you receive your impression.
- In what ways do you think your impression differs from the sense of himself that the Pardoner seems to project?

671 **him** the Summoner

672 **compeer** companion

675 **bar to him a stif burdoun** sang the bass part loudly [As this is a love song there could be a suggestion in this phrase of a homosexual affair between the Summoner and the Pardoner.]

676 **trompe** trumpet

678 **strike of flex** hank of flax [i.e. dry and lifeless]

679 **ounces** small gatherings, bunches, rats' tails [Long hair was forbidden to clerics, suggesting that this Pardoner was not officially licensed, or else did not care about the rules.]

681 **colpons** sections

682 **for jolitee** for the sake of his appearance

684 **al of the newe jet** in the very latest fashion

685 **Dischevelee ... al bare** with his hair all dishevelled, he rode bareheaded except for his skull cap

686 **glaringe eyen** [Glaring eyes were thought of as the mark of a libertine, and the hare was spoken of as a creature that slept with open eyes. It was also considered a hermaphrodite.]

687 **vernicle** [A medal with the representation of Veronica's veil, with which she wiped Christ's face as he was carrying his cross. It was a sign of having made a pilgrimage to Rome. 'Vernicle' is a diminutive of 'Veronica'.]

689 **bretful** brimful

690 **as smal as hath a goot** as weak as a goat's [i.e. thin and high]

691 **ne nevere sholde have** nor ever would have [i.e. he never would become sexually mature]

692 **late** lately, newly

692 **fro Berwik into Ware** from Berwick to Ware [i.e. from one end of the country to the other]

The Pardoner's appearance and behaviour are introduced in this description from the General Prologue.

    With him ther rood a gentil Pardoner
Of Rouncivale, his freend and his compeer,
That streight was comen fro the court of Rome.
Ful loude he soong 'Com hider, love, to me!'
This Somonour bar to him a stif burdoun;   675
Was nevere trompe of half so greet a soun.
This Pardoner hadde heer as yelow as wex,
But smothe it heeng as dooth a strike of flex;
By ounces henge his lokkes that he hadde,
And therwith he his shuldres overspradde;   680
But thinne it lay, by colpons oon and oon.
But hood, for jolitee, wered he noon,
For it was trussed up in his walet.
Him thoughte he rood al of the newe jet;
Dischevelee, save his cappe, he rood al bare.   685
Swiche glaringe eyen hadde he as an hare.
A vernicle hadde he sowed upon his cappe.
His walet lay biforn him in his lappe,
Bretful of pardoun, comen from Rome al hoot.
A voys he hadde as smal as hath a goot.   690
No berd hadde he, ne nevere sholde have;
As smothe it was as it were late shave.
I trowe he were a gelding or a mare.
But of his craft, fro Berwik into Ware,
Ne was ther swich another pardoner.   695

- Chaucer as narrator can be heard in these lines, but his voice is not always the same. At what points do you think the tone of voice changes? Write down as exactly as you can what you think the changes are, and then compare your conclusions with a partner.
- What do you think Chaucer might mean by 'noble' (line 710)?
- Write a paragraph describing the Pardoner as Chaucer presents him in these lines.

696	**male** pouch, luggage
	pilwe-beer pillow case
698	**gobet of the seil** piece of the sail
700	**til Jhesu Crist him hente** til Jesus Christ took him (into the boat) [For the episode of walking on the water see St Matthew's Gospel, chapter 6.]
701	**crois of latoun ful of stones** a brass cross [Latoun is an alloy of tin and copper that looks like gold but is base metal. The stones or gems are also presumably false.]
704	**person** parson
	upon lond in the country
706	**gat in monthes tweye** received in two months

707	**feyned** pretended, false
708	**made the person and the peple his apes** made fools of the parson and people (congregation)
709	**atte laste** finally
710	**noble ecclesiaste** a fine cleric
711	**lessoun or a storie** the readings from the Bible that take place during mass
712	**alderbest** best of all
	offertorie [that part of the mass, sung by priest and people, during which they made their offering]
713	**affile** smooth
716	**murierly** more merrily

In spite of his appearance the Pardoner can impress people and gain a hold over them. He is not a priest, but plays a part in the life of the church that might have seemed priestlike to ignorant people.

For in his male he hadde a pilwe-beer,
Which that he seyde was Oure Lady veil:
He seyde he hadde a gobet of the seil
That Seint Peter hadde, whan that he wente
Upon the see, til Jhesu Crist him hente. 700
He hadde a crois of latoun ful of stones,
And in a glas he hadde pigges bones.
But with thise relikes, whan that he fond
A povre person dwellinge upon lond,
Upon a day he gat him moore moneye 705
Than that the person gat in monthes tweye;
And thus, with feyned flaterye and japes,
He made the person and the peple his apes.
But trewely to tellen atte laste,
He was in chirche a noble ecclesiaste. 710
Wel koude he rede a lessoun or a storie,
But alderbest he song an offertorie;
For wel he wiste, whan that song was songe,
He moste preche and wel affile his tonge
To winne silver, as he ful wel koude;
Therefore he song the murierly and loude. 715

The Pardoner as depicted in the Ellesmere manuscript. This was written and decorated in the fifteenth century, but reproduced the style of dress of the 1380s

The Doctor has just finished his Tale which ends with the death of a beautiful virgin, killed by her father to frustrate a plot by a wicked judge to make her a concubine.

- Read the first 12 lines aloud, with your ordinary pronunciation. Try to get the general meaning before you start to study the detailed notes below. When you have studied them, read the lines aloud again.
- The Host does not mention spiritual gifts in line 9. Why do you think this might be?
- What do you think is the Host's real opinion of the Doctor's story, and of the Doctor? See lines 16-22.

1	**gan swere as he were wood** began to swear as if he were mad
2	**Harrow! Alas!** [*literally:* 'Help']
	by nailes and by blood by the nails (that fixed Christ to the cross) and by (Christ's) blood. [We are introduced to blasphemy at the very outset. There is much more to come.]
3	**cherl** wretch
	justise judge
5	**thise** such [i.e. such false judges]
	advocats lawyers [or perhaps 'hangers on']
6	**Algate** all the same
	sely blessed, innocent [later to take on the modern meaning 'silly']
7	**to deere boughte she beautee** she paid too high a price for her beauty
8	**al day** always
9	**yiftes of Fortune and of Nature** gifts of wealth or rank, and of beauty and intelligence
13	**bothe yiftes** [i.e. the gifts of Fortune and Nature]
14	**han** receive
	prow benefit
15	**myn owene maister deere** my own dear master [the Physician who has just told his Tale]
17	**is no fors** does not matter

18	**cors** body
19	**eek** also
	urinals chamber pots [Physicians often made a diagnosis of illness by examining the patient's urine.]
	jurdones wine flasks
20	**ypocras** spiced wine
	galiones a drink
19-20	[The Host's language suggests an uneducated man stretching his knowledge to the limit. 'Ypocras' echoes the name of Hippocrates, who greatly influenced the development of medicine in ancient Greece and for many centuries afterwards. 'Galiones' is not found elsewhere; the context suggests a drink, and the name echoes Galen, a profoundly influential Arab physician of the early middle ages. 'Jurdones' were possibly named after the River Jordan, because of the common practice of bringing home water from the Jordan after a pilgrimage. There are distant but clear connections with health in all three references; the Host, as an inn-keeper, would know all about the healthful properties of drink.]
21	**boyste** box
	letuarie medicine

The Host launches into a fierce diatribe against the injustice of the closing events of the Doctor's Tale. He then thanks the Doctor for his Tale.

Oure Hooste gan to swere as he were wood;
'Harrow!' quod he, 'by nailes and by blood!
This was a fals cherl and a fals justise.
As shameful deeth as herte may devise
Come to thise juges and hire advocats!   5
Algate this sely maide is slain, allas!
Allas, to deere boughte she beautee!
Wherfore I seye al day that men may see
That yiftes of Fortune and of Nature
Been cause of deeth to many a creature.   10
Hire beautee was hire deth, I dar wel sayn.
Allas, so pitously as she was slain!
Of bothe yiftes that I speke of now
Men han ful ofte moore for harm than prow.
But trewely, myn owene maister deere,   15
This is a pitous tale for to heere.
But nathelees, passe over, is no fors.
I pray to God so save thy gentil cors,
And eek thine urinals and thy jurdones,
Thyn ypocras, and eek thy galiones,   20
And every boyste ful of thy letuarie;
God blesse hem, and oure lady Seinte Marie.

- Do you think the Host's words in lines 25-33 tell us anything more about the Host's reactions to the Doctor's Tale?
- What impression of the Pardoner do you receive from lines 32-42?
- Look back at the section on Chaucer's language (page 8), and then read these lines aloud, trying to get the rhythm right, and paying particular attention to the pronunciation of the final 'e'.

23 **So moot I theen** [There is no exact equivalent; the sense is given by a phrase such as 'As I live and breathe'.]

24 **prelat** high-ranking church dignitary [a bishop or higher]

Seint Ronyan [a mysterious name, perhaps Ronan or Ninian, but possibly another of the Host's 'near misses', as in lines 19-20]

25 **I kan nat speke in terme** I cannot use your technical language [though he seems to have tried]

26 **woot** know

doost make

erme grieve

27 **cardynacle** heart attack [This is another 'near miss' or malapropism. The term in Chaucer's time was 'cardiacle', and the insertion of an 'n' suggests a pun on 'cardinal', although it may just be an error in copying the manuscript at some stage.]

28 **By Corpus bones** by God's bones [This is one of the Host's favourite oaths. It is short for 'By Corpus Domini', 'By the body of Christ', a strong term amounting to blasphemy unless uttered seriously in a worthy context. The Host's version is a kind of abbreviation suggesting that he does not have enough Latin to understand the full meaning: his version means literally 'By body bones'.]

but I have triacle unless I have a remedy ['Triacle' is the origin of the modern word 'treacle'.]

30 **anon** immediately

myrie merry

31 **lost** grief-stricken, broken

32 **beel ami** good fellow [The usage here is slightly contemptuous: the expression itself is polite, but in view of what comes later the Host seems already to have formed a poor opinion of the Pardoner.]

33 **japes** jokes

35 **alestake** inn sign [Pubs were identified by the long stake or stick placed outside them with some evergreen foliage on the end.]

37 **gentils** gentle folk, polite people

gonne to crye began to cry out, did cry out

38 **ribaudye** ribaldry, filthy jokes

39 **moral thing** something teaching a moral lesson

leere learn

40 **wit** practical wisdom

37-40 [There is evidence that some at least of the pilgrims share the Host's reservations about Pardoners. They expect the worst – some low tale fuelled by drink. The Pardoner's insistence on stopping for a drink before telling his tale suggests they are right.]

41 **I graunte, ywis** I certainly agree

moot must

42 **honest** decent

The Host pays extravagant compliments to the Doctor, though he sometimes trips over his words in an apparent attempt to appear well informed. He calls upon the Pardoner to tell an amusing tale, to the dismay of the pilgrims, who seem alarmed by the Pardoner's need for a drink before he starts.

So moot I theen, thou art a propre man,
And lyk a prelat, by Seint Ronyan!
Seyde I nat wel? I kan nat speke in terme;   25
But wel I woot thou doost myn herte to erme,
That I almoost have caught a cardynacle.
By Corpus bones! but I have triacle,
Or elles a draughte of moiste and corny ale,
Or but I heere anon a myrie tale,   30
Myn herte is lost for pitee of this maide.
Thou beel ami, thou Pardoner,' he saide,
'Telle us som mirthe or japes right anon.'
    'It shal be doon,' quod he, 'by Seint Ronyon!
But first,' quod he, 'heere at this alestake   35
I wol bothe drinke, and eten of a cake.'
    But right anon thise gentils gonne to crye,
'Nay, lat him telle us of no ribaudye!
Telle us som moral thing, that we may leere
Som wit, and thanne wol we gladly heere.'   40
    'I graunte, ywis,' quod he, 'but I moot thinke
Upon som honest thing while that I drinke.'

- What do you think is the Pardoner's attitude towards his congregation when he addresses them, and what is his attitude to the pilgrims?
- Read lines 49-60 again and note all the indications that you think might suggest the Pardoner is 'official'; are there any indications that he might be a self-appointed imposter? List the points for and against.
- Write a paragraph describing the Pardoner's character as it is revealed in these opening lines.

43 **Lordinges** gentlemen

44 **I peyne me to han an hauteyn speche** I take care to adopt an imposing way of speaking

45 **as round as gooth a belle** as clearly [possibly smoothly] as a bell sounds

46 **kan al by rote** know by heart

48 ***Radix malorum est Cupiditas*** love of money is the root of all evil [The Pardoner's text is from St Paul's First Epistle to Timothy, chapter 6. The Pardoner has only one sermon, on a text spectacularly opposed to his own way of life. He refers to his text again on line 114 and quotes the Latin again on line 140.]

49 **pronounce** announce

   whennes whence, from where

50 **bulles** official church documents [i.e. any official document, not necessarily papal documents]

   alle and some every one of them

51 **Oure lige lordes seel on my patente** the Bishop's seal [possibly the Pope's seal] on my licence to preach

52 **my body to warente** to protect myself

54 **Me to destourbe of** to hinder me from

55 **telle I forth my tales** say my piece, say what I have to say [This is followed by a long section of complacent self-revelation.]

59 **To saffron with my predicacioun** to season, or to add colour to, my preaching

60 **hem** them [contemptuous]

61 **cristal stones** long glass boxes [possibly glass-lidded boxes kept to display relics]

62 **cloutes** cloths

63 **as wenen they echoon** as they all believe

64 **in latoun a sholder-boon** a clavicle (shoulder blade) in a setting made from an alloy of copper and zinc [The ignorant might well think this alloy to be gold.]

65 **an hooly Jewes sheep** [a vague and off-hand reference suggesting something to do with the Bible]

'And thanne my bulles shewe I, alle and some'

20

Having presumably had his drink, the Pardoner launches dramatically into what he wants to say. He is still some distance away from his tale. He describes his approach to preaching and his methods. He is keen to establish his good standing as a visiting preacher, but goes on to give such an unlikely list of references that he raises suspicion, and finishes with a contemptuous list of the 'relics' he has for sale.

'Lordinges,' quod he, 'in chirches whan I preche,
I peyne me to han an hauteyn speche,
And ringe it out as round as gooth a belle,   45
For I kan al by rote that I telle.
My theme is alwey oon, and evere was—
Radix malorum est Cupiditas.
   First I pronounce whennes that I come,
And thanne my bulles shewe I, alle and some.   50
Oure lige lordes seel on my patente,
That shewe I first, my body to warente,
That no man be so boold, ne preest ne clerk,
Me to destourbe of Cristes hooly werk.
And after that thanne telle I forth my tales.   55
Bulles of popes and of cardinales,
Of patriarkes and bishopes I shewe,
And in Latin I speke a wordes fewe,
To saffron with my predicacioun,
And for to stire hem to devocioun.   60
Thanne shewe I forth my longe cristal stones,
Ycrammed ful of cloutes and of bones,—
Relikes been they, as wenen they echoon.
Thanne have I in latoun a sholder-boon
Which that was of an hooly Jewes sheep.   65

The Pardoner knows the worldly needs of his victims, and offers them healthy live-stock and a cure for many human ills, if they buy his remedies.

- The Pardoner's 'offers' to his hearers seem to grow more dubious by the minute. Do you think that in these lines he is reporting what he says to his congregation, or talking to the pilgrims, perhaps after a little too much to drink? Explain your view in detail.
- Whoever his audience may be, the Pardoner has said that he delivers only one stock sermon. Read aloud the three sentences that make up lines 80-5, 86-90 and 91-8. How would you describe the language? How much does he expect his audience to take seriously? What do you think would be the effect of such statements on his audience?
- Re-read lines 91-8 aloud. What do you think would be the likely effect of what he says on the guilty, especially in front of people they know?

66	**Goode men** Dear brothers [a standard opening to a sermon]
67	**wasshe** washed or dipped
68	**swelle** should swell [fall ill]
69	**That any worm hath ete, or worm ystonge** That has eaten any [harmful] creature [e.g. a liver-fluke] or that has been bitten/stung. ['Worm' in Chaucer's day meant roughly what we might mean by 'creepy-crawly', and could include snakes.]
71	**hool** whole, healed
72	**pokkes ... scabbe** pox and scab [skin diseases of sheep that affect their wool as well as their health]
74	**taak kep** take note
75	**the good-man that the beestes oweth** the householder who owns the beasts
76	**wyke** week
78	**thilke** that same **eldres** forefathers
79	**stoor** livestock
82	**potage** soup
84-5	**Though ...two or thre** even though he knew the truth about her infidelity, even if she had slept with two or three priests
86	**Heere is a miteyn eek** here also is a mitten [used for sowing seed by hand]
89	**whete or otes** wheat or oats
90	**So that** as long as **pens** pence **grotes** coins worth 4 old pence [quite a large amount of money]
92	**wight** person
94	**yshriven** confessed
96	**cokewold** cuckold
97	**ne** nor **grace** spiritual strength

The Pardoner continues to give a clear and apparently quite honest sample of his sermon.

"Goode men," I seye, "taak of my wordes keep;
If that this boon be wasshe in any welle,
If cow, or calf, or sheep, or oxe swelle
That any worm hath ete, or worm ystonge,
Taak water of that welle and wassh his tonge,   70
And it is hool anon; and forthermoore,
Of pokkes and of scabbe and every soore
Shal every sheep be hool that of this welle
Drinketh a draughte. Taak kep eek what I telle:
If that the good-man that the beestes oweth   75
Wol every wyke, er that the cok him croweth,
Fastinge, drinken of this welle a draughte,
As thilke hooly Jew oure eldres taughte,
His beestes and his stoor shal multiplie.
    And, sires, also it heeleth jalousie;   80
For though a man be falle in jalous rage,
Lat maken with this water his potage,
And nevere shal he moore his wif mistriste,
Though he the soothe of hir defaute wiste,
Al had she taken prestes two or thre.   85
    Heere is a miteyn eek, that ye may se.
He that his hand wol putte in this mitayn,
He shal have multiplying of his grain,
Whan he hath sowen, be it whete or otes,
So that he offre pens, or elles grotes.   90
    Goode men and wommen, o thing warne I yow:
If any wight be in this chirche now
That hath doon sinne horrible, that he
Dar nat for shame of it yshriven be,
Or any womman, be she yong or old,   95
That hath ymaad hir housbonde cokewold,
Swich folk shal have no power ne no grace
To offren to my relikes in this place.

- Who do you think experiences the joy mentioned in line 113?
- What do you think could be the Pardoner's reason for making the declaration in lines 114-118?
- Look back over the Pardoner's Prologue and make a list of the material things he mentions. Then make a list of the spiritual things listed in this section of the work.
- The Pardoner reduces everlasting damnation to 'goon a-blakeberied' (line 120). What in your view is the effect of this, bearing in mind his function in the church?
- What impression of the Pardoner do you receive from the action he describes in line 127?
- Who do you think are the 'bretheren' mentioned in line 130?

99	**out of** innocent of
101	**assoille** absolve
103	**gaude** trick
	wonne profited
104	**An hundred mark** sum of money equivalent to £66.66 [A vast income at that time. See lines 705-6 of the Pardoner's portrait in The General Prologue, where he is described as receiving more in a day than a poor parson got in two months.]

105	**lyk a clerk** like a cleric
106	**lewed** unlearned, ignorant
110	**bekke** nod
111	**berne** barn [Lines 110-11 give a clear picture of the Pardoner's actions, but also suggest a parody of another dove – the symbol of the Holy Spirit. This is a subtle form of blasphemy which would be wrong in a spiritual and honest Pardoner. Here Chaucer is perhaps leading the audience towards the more open blasphemy of the Tale.]
112	**yerne** busily
114	**bisynesse** activity
115	**free** eager
120	**soules goon a-blakeberied** souls wandering aimlessly [i.e. damned]
123	**Som ... flaterye** some to please people and to flatter them
124	**avaunced** promoted
125	**veyne** vain, empty
127	**him** them, or 'whoever it is'
128	**asterte** avoid
130	**trespased** offended or opposed

'I stonde lyk a clerk in my pulpet'

The Pardoner explains that this is exactly how he preaches, and he gives an account of his style of delivery. He also shows how he uses any technique or approach to wring money out of people.

And whoso findeth him out of swich blame,
He wol come up and offre in Goddes name, 100
And I assoille him by the auctoritee
Which that by bulle ygraunted was to me."
  By this gaude have I wonne, yeer by yeer,
An hundred mark sith I was pardoner.
I stonde lyk a clerk in my pulpet, 105
And whan the lewed peple is doun yset,
I preche so as ye han herd bifoore,
And telle an hundred false japes moore.
Thanne peyne I me to strecche forth the nekke,
And est and west upon the peple I bekke, 110
As dooth a dowve sittinge on a berne.
Mine handes and my tonge goon so yerne
That it is joye to se my bisynesse.
Of avarice and of swich cursednesse
Is al my preching, for to make hem free 115
To yeven hir pens, and namely unto me.
For myn entente is nat but for to winne,
And nothing for correccioun of sinne.
I rekke nevere, whan that they been beried,
Though that hir soules goon a-blakeberied. 120
For certes, many a predicacioun
Comth ofte time of yvel entencioun;
Som for plesance of folk and flaterye,
To been avaunced by ypocrisye,
And som for veyne glorie, and som for hate. 125
For whan I dar noon oother weyes debate,
Thanne wol I stinge him with my tonge smerte
In preching, so that he shal nat asterte
To been defamed falsly, if that he
Hath trespased to my bretheren or to me. 130

- The Pardoner takes his way of life very seriously. What is your impression of him in lines 137-48?
- How would you describe the tone of lines 149-60?
- What effect do you think the declaration in lines 153-60 would have on the pilgrims?
- Read lines 137-60 aloud, as faithfully as you can to the original pronunciation. To what extent do you think these lines show the Pardoner as an effective speaker?

131   **his** [whoever is his target from the pulpit. The victim is not named but clearly identified to the congregation.]

134   **quyte** pay back, get even with
      us Pardoners

135   **hewe** appearance

137   **But ... devise** [This is a sort of headline, not uncommon in medieval verse, and perhaps in medieval sermons. Line 148 has the effect of closing the section that opens on this line.]

138   **coveitise** covetousness, desire for gain

140   *Radix ... Cupiditas* [See note to line 48.]

144   **twynne** depart from, give up

148   **Of this ... suffise** this should be enough on this subject

149   **ensanples** examples [a technical term from the medieval art of preaching]

150   **agoon** past, ago

152   **reporte** repeat
      holde hold, or keep in mind [This is why preachers used so many examples from well-known tales, but the Pardoner does not mind expressing a poor opinion of his congregations.]

153   **trowe ye** do you think

154   **for I teche** through my teaching

155   **wifully** deliberately, on purpose

156   **Nay, nay ... trewely!** no, no, that was never what I intended, honestly!

157   **sondry landes** different countries [The sense is 'anywhere'.]

159   **make baskettes** [This is a reference to St Paul the Hermit (not St Paul the Apostle), who earned his living weaving baskets.]

The Pardoner expresses professional solidarity with his fellow Pardoners. He describes his activities, the side effects they might have in bringing some people to repent their sins, and his determination to escape poverty.

For though I telle noght his propre name,
Men shal wel knowe that it is the same
By signes, and by othere circumstances.
Thus quyte I folk that doon us displesances;
Thus spitte I out my venym under hewe   135
Of hoolinesse, to semen hooly and trewe.
    But shortly myn entente I wol devise:
I preche of no thing but for coveitise.
Therfore my theme is yet, and evere was,
Radix malorum est Cupiditas.   140
Thus kan I preche again that same vice
Which that I use, and that is avarice.
But though myself be gilty in that sinne,
Yet kan I maken oother folk to twynne
From avarice, and soore to repente.   145
But that is nat my principal entente;
I preche nothing but for coveitise.
Of this mateere it oghte ynogh suffise.
    Thanne telle I hem ensamples many oon
Of olde stories longe time agoon.   150
For lewed peple loven tales olde;
Swiche thinges kan they wel reporte and holde.
What, trowe ye that whiles I may preche,
And winne gold and silver for I teche,
That I wol live in poverte wilfully?   155
Nay, nay, I thoghte it nevere, trewely!
For I wol preche and begge in sondry landes;
I wol nat do no labour with mine handes,
Ne make baskettes, and live therby,
By cause I wol nat beggen idelly.   160

- The Pardoner asserts his will very clearly in lines 161-6 (he has asserted it negatively in lines 155-60 above). How far would you say that he has consciously chosen to live like this?
- Can you see evidence of the Pardoner's enjoyment of what he is saying in these lines? Write a paragraph summarising the evidence.
- Look back over the Pardoner's Prologue. What motives do you think drove him to make this extraordinary public confession? What kind of morals does he possess?
- We, the readers, know that the Pardoner deceives his congregations, but they do not. How far would you think it possible for a corrupt preacher to move his audience to genuine repentance? Does this corruption make a mockery of his moral message?

161   **countrefete** imitate [As a cleric the Pardoner was supposed to imitate the apostles, and, through the apostles, Christ. The reference to the apostles might have been suggested by the reference to St Paul the Hermit in line 159, who was not St Paul the Apostle. The confusion might suggest that the Pardoner is used to making false connections without being challenged by congregations that knew no better.]

162   **wolle** wool (for clothing)

163   **Al were it yeven of** even if were given by

         povereste poorest

165   **sterve for famine** die of starvation ['Starve' still survives in some areas as a dialect word meaning 'die'. After Chaucer's time it acquired the specialised meaning 'die from lack of food'.]

171-2   **By God ... youre liking** By God, I intend to tell you something that you are bound to enjoy, unless you are unreasonable [This double appeal, to God and to reason, suggests some of the strange contradictions in this character. In Chaucer's time reason was not thought sufficient: humans needed faith in God as well.]

175   **am wont to** usually, or 'am in the habit of'

         winne make money

176   **hoold youre pees!** be quiet, pay attention

The Pardoner ends his Prologue with a kind of manifesto declaring what he wants from life. He talks of the lengths he is prepared to go in order to get what he wants, and then asserts that his moral tale is something that, as rational people, they are bound to like.

I wol noon of the apostles countrefete;
I wol have moneie, wolle, chese, and whete,
Al were it yeven of the povereste page,
Or of the povereste widwe in a village,
Al sholde hir children sterve for famine.   165
Nay, I wol drinke licour of the vine,
And have a joly wenche in every toun.
But herkneth, lordinges, in conclusioun:
Youre liking is that I shal telle a tale.
Now have I dronke a draughte of corny ale,   170
By God, I hope I shal yow telle a thing
That shal by reson been at youre liking.
For though myself be a ful vicious man,
A moral tale yet I yow telle kan,
Which I am wont to preche for to winne.   175
Now hoold youre pees! my tale I wol biginne.'

The Pardoner condemns the sin of swearing by invoking parts of Christ's body – e.g. 'by God's arms' – because they were seen as re-crucifying Christ in blasphemy. The reference to Jews is an example of the routine anti-semitism of the day: Jews were regarded as Christ-killers.

- If riot, gambling, etc, are the ritual of devil worship (line 183), where does the Pardoner locate the devil's temple?
- Read aloud lines 177-98, trying to feel the sweep of the language as the young debauchees and their activities are introduced.
- How effective as a sermon would you say this section is? Look closely at the detail of the text, and write a paragraph on how you think the pilgrims or a congregation might be affected.

177	**whilom** once, or 'once upon a time'
178	**haunteden folye** practised folly [The sense is that they 'went in for' folly. Folly means here not merely something foolish or ill-advised but something disastrous and self-destructive.]
179	**As riot, hasard, stywes** such as debauchery, gambling, brothels
180	**giternes** lutes
181	**dees** dice
182	**over hir might** beyond their capacity
185	**superfluitee abhominable** beastly excess
186	**othes** swearing, blasphemy
187	**grisly** appalling, terrible
188	**totere** tear to pieces
189	**hem thoughte** it seemed to them
	rente tore
190	**lough** laughed
191	**tombesteres** dancing girls
192	**fetys and smale** graceful and slender
	frutesteres fruit-sellers
193	**baudes** pimps

	wafereres sellers of sweets and confectionery [often thought of as go-betweens in illicit love affairs]
194-5	**the verray develes officeres/ To kindle** the true servants of the devil/ Whose job is to kindle
196	**annexed** bound up with
197	**The hooly writ** the Bible [See Ephesians, chapter 5 verse 18.]
198	**luxurie** lechery
199	**Looth** Lot [See Genesis, chapter 19 verses 30-6.]
	unkindely unnaturally
200	**unwitingly** unknowingly, not knowing what he was doing
201	**nyste** did not know [This word is a combination of the negative 'ne' and 'wyste' meaning 'knew'.]
202	**whoso wel the stories soghte** [as] whoever looked through the stories carefully [would know]
204	**heeste** order
205	**ful giltelees** though he was completely innocent

The Pardoner starts his story but very soon digresses into a long sermon on sin, specifically the kind of dreadful acts – particularly lustful ones – that people commit when drunk. He does not return to his narrative until line 375.

In Flaundres whilom was a compaignye
Of yonge folk that haunteden folye,
As riot, hasard, stywes, and tavernes,
Where as with harpes, lutes, and giternes,   180
They daunce and pleyen at dees bothe day and night,
And eten also and drinken over hir might,
Thurgh which they doon the devel sacrifise
Withinne that develes temple, in cursed wise,
By superfluitee abhominable.   185
Hir othes been so grete and so dampnable
That it is grisly for to heere hem swere.
Oure blissed Lordes body they totere—
Hem thoughte that Jewes rente him noght ynough;
And ech of hem at otheres sinne lough.   190
And right anon thanne comen tombesteres
Fetys and smale, and yonge frutesteres,
Singeres with harpes, baudes, wafereres,
Whiche been the verray develes officeres
To kindle and blowe the fyr of lecherye,   195
That is annexed unto glotonye.
The hooly writ take I to my witnesse
That luxurie is in wyn and dronkenesse.
    Lo, how that dronken Looth, unkindely,
Lay by his doghtres two, unwitingly;   200
So dronke he was, he nyste what he wroghte.
    Herodes, whoso wel the stories soghte,
Whan he of wyn was repleet at his feeste,
Right at his owene table he yaf his heeste
To sleen the Baptist John, ful giltelees.   205

- If the sin of Adam and Eve – eating the fruit of the Tree of Knowledge – was caused by gluttony, how broadly would you define gluttony? Read the account in the Book of Genesis, chapter 3. (Lines 219-25 are an adaptation of a passage from St Jerome's book 'Against Jovinian'.)
- Look at lines 212-15 and 226-9. What is the effect of these sections in the Pardoner's sermon?
- How would you describe the tone of the Pardoner's comments on gluttony in lines 227-34?

206 **Senec** Seneca [a Roman writer of the first century AD, well known in the Middle Ages]

209 **dronkelewe** drunk

210-11 **But that ...dronkenesse** Except that madness, happening in some poor creature, lasts longer than drunkenness

212-14 **O glotonye ... dampnacioun** [The Pardoner is using a convention of preaching. The repeated 'O' at the beginning of these lines is intended to draw attention to their content. This rhetorical device was known technically as 'apostrophe'.]

213 **confusion** ruin

215 **boght us with his blood again** redeemed us

216-17 **Lo, how ... vileynye** to put it briefly, see how dearly [expensively]

redeemed was that cursed wrong-doing

218 **for glotonye** because of gluttony

221 **it is no drede** there is no doubt

222 **fasted** abstained
as I rede as I read [in Genesis 3]

224 **deffended** forbidden

227 **wiste a man** if one knew

229 **mesurable** moderate

233 **swinke** labour

234 **deyntee** delicate, choice
mete food

235 **Paul** [reference to St Paul's First Epistle to the Corinthians, chapter 6 verse 13]
wel kanstow trete you deal well [with this matter]

236 **wombe** belly

'O glotonye, full of cursednesse!'

The Pardoner continues his sermon with a fierce attack first on drunkenness and then on gluttony, of which drunkenness is a part. He claims that all sin arises from gluttony, because the sin of Adam and Eve arose from their wish to eat the apple from the Tree of Knowledge.

Senec seith a good word doutelees;
He seith he kan no difference finde
Bitwix a man that is out of his minde
And a man which that is dronkelewe,
But that woodnesse, yfallen in a shrewe,   210
Persevereth lenger than doth dronkenesse.
O glotonye, ful of cursednesse!
O cause first of oure confusioun!
O original of oure dampnacioun,
Til Crist hadde boght us with his blood again!   215
Lo, how deere, shortly for to sayn,
Aboght was thilke cursed vileynye—
Corrupt was al this world for glotonye.
    Adam oure fader, and his wyf also,
Fro Paradis to labour and to wo   220
Were driven for that vice, it is no drede.
For whil that Adam fasted, as I rede,
He was in Paradis; and whan that he
Eet of the fruit deffended on the tree,
Anon he was out cast to wo and peyne.   225
O glotonye, on thee wel oghte us pleyne!
O, wiste a man how manye maladies
Folwen of excesse and of glotonies,
He wolde been the moore mesurable
Of his diete, sittinge at his table.   230
Allas, the shorte throte, the tendre mouth,
Maketh that est and west and north and south,
In erthe, in eir, in water, men to swinke
To gete a glotoun deyntee mete and drinke.
Of this matiere, o Paul, wel kanstow trete: 235
'Mete unto wombe, and wombe eek unto mete,
Shal God destroyen bothe,' as Paulus seith.

In line 253 there is some medieval philosophy: accidents are the exterior qualities of anything, those qualities that are perceived by the various senses; substance is the essential nature of the thing, not perceptible to the senses.

• What do you think the Pardoner might mean by 'by my feith' (line 238)?
• Re-read lines 255-7 aloud, preferably with a partner. Then write a paragraph describing the effects of the sounds in the verse.

239 **dede** act

241 **privee** latrine

243 **The apostel** St Paul [in the Epistle to the Philippians, chapter 3 verses 18-19]

244 **walken** behave [with the sense of 'live their lives']

247 **of whiche** whose [i.e. those who behave like this]

248 **cod** belly [*literally:* bag. This line is another example of 'apostrophe', with an irregular rhythm for effect.]

251 **to finde** to provide or satisfy

253 **And turnen substaunce into accident** [This is a blasphemous reference to consecration at mass, when the accidents of the bread and wine remain the same but their substance is transubstantiated into the body and blood of Christ. Here the Pardoner suggests that cooks labour to produce a sort of reverse effect.]

254 **likerous talent** lecherous appetite

256 **mary** marrow

257 **That** anything that

golet gullet

swoote sweet

258 **Of** from

259 **his sauce ymaked by delit** his [the glutton's] sauce shall be made for his delight

260 **yet** constantly

261 **delices** delights

262 **deed** spiritually dead [Lines 261-2 are a reference to St Paul's First Epistle to Timothy, chapter 5 verse 6.]

The Pardoner develops his attack on gluttony, dwelling first on the revolting aspects of self-indulgence and then on the delights of food and drink.

Allas, a foul thing is it, by my feith,
To seye this word, and fouler is the dede,
Whan man so drinketh of the white and rede   240
That of his throte he maketh his privee,
Thurgh thilke cursed superfluitee.
  The apostel weping seith ful pitously,
'Ther walken manye of whiche yow toold have I—
I seye it now weping, with pitous vois—   245
That they been enemys of Cristes crois,
Of whiche the ende is deeth, wombe is hir god.'
O wombe! O bely! O stinking cod,
Fulfilled of dong and of corrupcioun!
At either ende of thee foul is the soun.   250
How greet labour and cost is thee to finde!
Thise cookes, how they stampe, and streyne, and grinde,
And turnen substaunce into accident,
To fulfille al thy likerous talent!
Out of the harde bones knokke they   255
The mary, for they caste noght awey
That may go thurgh the golet softe and swoote.
Of spicerie of leef and bark and roote
Shal been his sauce ymaked by delit,
To make him yet a newer appetit.   260
But certes, he that haunteth swiche delices
Is deed, whil that he liveth in tho vices.

- Bearing in mind that the Pardoner's declared motive has nothing to do with reforming his listeners, do you think his diatribe against drunkenness is effective? In what ways?
- What is the effect of the sudden change in lines 287-92? What kind of acts is the Pardoner recommending?

264	**striving** quarrelling
266	**artow** art thou
268	**Sampsoun, Sampsoun** [apparently an imitation of the noise of snoring]
269	**nevere** [must be pronounced 'ne'er' here to fit the rhythm. The reference to Sampson is to be found in the Book of Judges 13.]
270	**a stiked swyn** a stuck [slaughtered] pig
271	**al thyn honeste cure** all your self respect [cure in the sense of 'care']
272	**sepulture** interment, burial
273	**discrecioun** judgment
275	**conseil** secret
	it is no drede there is no doubt
276	**kepe yow fro** keep yourselves away from
277	**namely** especially
	Lepe [in Spain, near Cadiz]
278	**to selle** for sale, on sale
	Chepe Cheapside [a market in the City of London]
279-80	**This wyn ... faste by** Spanish wines will somehow, on their journey to

England, find their way into French wines, which they encounter on the way [Chaucer's family were wine importers, and this may well be a sly reference to the adulteration of expensive French wine with inferior Spanish wine.]

281	**fumositee** [People thought that the fumes of alcohol, rising directly from the stomach to the brain, caused drunkenness.]
283	**weneth** thinks
284-5	**He is ...Burdeux toun** betrayed by strong wine, he does not know where he is; he is not at Rochelle, nor at Bordeaux, but in Lepe (where the wine is much stronger) [There is a strong suggestion of an insider joke here; it seems unlikely that the Pardoner's usual audience would understand this reference.]
288	**soverein** principal
	dar I seye I say without hesitation
290	**verray** true
	omnipotent almighty, all-powerful
292	**leere** learn

The attack now concentrates on drunkenness, combining pictures of someone stupefied by drink with jokes about the unreliable quality of the wine. There is also a warning that great things were achieved in Old Testament times only by those who put a sober and prayerful trust in God.

A lecherous thing is wyn, and dronkenesse
Is ful of striving and of wrecchednesse.
O dronke man, disfigured is thy face,   265
Sour is thy breeth, foul artow to embrace,
And thurgh thy dronke nose semeth the soun
As though thou seydest ay 'Sampsoun, Sampsoun!'
And yet, God woot, Sampsoun drank nevere no wyn.
Thou fallest as it were a stiked swyn;   270
Thy tonge is lost, and al thyn honeste cure;
For dronkenesse is verray sepulture
Of mannes wit and his discrecioun.
In whom that drinke hath dominacioun
He kan no conseil kepe, it is no drede.   275
Now kepe yow fro the white and fro the rede,
And namely fro the white wyn of Lepe,
That is to selle in Fisshstrete or in Chepe.
This wyn of Spaigne crepeth subtilly
In othere wines, growinge faste by,   280
Of which ther riseth swich fumositee
That whan a man hath dronken draughtes thre,
And weneth that he be at hoom in Chepe,
He is in Spaigne, right at the toune of Lepe—
Nat at the Rochele, ne at Burdeux toun;   285
And thanne wol he seye 'Sampsoun, Sampsoun!'
   But herkneth, lordinges, o word, I yow preye,
That alle the soverein actes, dar I seye,
Of victories in the Olde Testament,
Thurgh verray God, that is omnipotent,   290
Were doon in abstinence and in preyere.
Looketh the Bible, and ther ye may it leere.

- What tone do you think the Pardoner adopts when he delivers line 299?
- Look at the list of sins and faults in lines 305-10. Examine the order and severity of the items, and write a paragraph on the effect achieved here.
- In what sense do you think the Pardoner is using the word 'blasphemy' in line 307?

293 **Looke** [A conventional word used to introduce an exemplum (example) in medieval sermons. The word is still used in a smilar way in conversation.]

Attila [A reference to Attila the Hun. Such a reference to a non-Christian would not have been common in medieval sermons, and would not have been universally approved. The Pardoner also refers to a Greek figure in line 317.]

294 **deyde** died

295 **ay** constantly, copiously

297 **aviseth yow right wel** consider carefully

298 **Lamuel** [See the Book of Proverbs, chapter 32 verses 4-5.]

301 **Of ... justise** of giving wine to those who administer justice [The reference is to the Book of Proverbs, chapter 31 verses 4-5.]

304 **Now wol ... hasardrye** Now I will forbid you to gamble

305 **mooder of lesinges** mother of lies

306 **forsweringes** perjuries, oath-breaking

308 **catel** goods, property

309 **repreeve** shame

311 **estaat** rank

317 **Stilboun** [This is a reference to a story concerning an ambassador called Chilon. The change in name might have been due to a mistake by the person who copied the manuscript. Chaucer would have read the story in *Policraticus*, a work on the follies of courts and courtiers by John of Salisbury, a twelfth century scholar.]

319 **Lacidomye** Sparta

to make hire alliaunce to make an alliance with them

322 **fond** found

'Hasard is verray mooder of lesinges,
And of deceite, and cursed forsweringes'

A list of examples follows, drawn from secular history and from the Bible, interspersed with an attack on the evils of gambling.

Looke, Attilla, the grete conquerour,
Deyde in his sleep with shame and dishonour,
Bledinge ay at his nose in dronkenesse.   295
A capitain sholde live in sobrenesse.
And over al this, aviseth yow right wel
What was comaunded unto Lamuel—
Nat Samuel, but Lamuel, seye I;
Redeth the Bible, and finde it expresly   300
Of wyn-yeving to hem that han justise.
Namoore of this, for it may wel suffise.
  And now that I have spoken of glotonye,
Now wol I yow deffenden hasardrye.
Hasard is verray mooder of lesinges,   305
And of deceite, and cursed forsweringes,
Blaspheme of Crist, manslaughtre, and wast also
Of catel and of time; and forthermo,
It is repreeve and contrarie of honour
For to ben holde a commune hasardour.   310
And ever the hyer he is of estaat,
The moore is he yholden desolaat.
If that a prince useth hasardrye,
In alle governaunce and policye
He is, as by commune opinioun,   315
Yholde the lasse in reputacioun.
  Stilboun, that was a wys embassadour,
Was sent to Corinthe, in ful greet honour,
Fro Lacidomye, to make hire alliaunce.
And whan he cam, him happede, par chaunce,   320
That alle the gretteste that were of that lond,
Pleyinge atte hasard he hem fond.

- The Pardoner is now well into his stride. Read aloud lines 323-34 to gain the sweep of the quotation from Stilboun.
- What reason is given for the condemnation of gambling? What unspoken grounds do you think a Christian sermon might have for disapproving of the activity? Bear in mind the Pardoner's way of life and activities.
- Look at lines 343-52. In what sense do you think that 'abhominable' could be seen as a Christian condemnation of false swearing of all sorts?

324	**he stal him** he went quietly, secretly
325	**lese** lose
326-7	**Ne I wol ... hasardours** [The spectacular collection of negatives in these lines is for strong emphasis.]
329	**me were levere die** I would rather die [*literally:* to me it were dearer to die]
333	**As by my ...tretee** Neither by my will nor by a treaty negotiated by me
336	**the book** [*Policraticus* again. See note to line 317.]
337	**sente him** [i.e. Demetrius]
338	**ther-biforn** previously
342	**to drive the day awey** to pass the time
345	**abhominable** [false etymology in Chaucer's day led people to think this came from the Latin words 'ab'

meaning 'away from' and 'homine' meaning 'man' – i.e. 'departing from man's nature'. This fits the sense, even though the true etymology, which suggests 'disgusting', is also a strong condemnation.]

346	**fals swering** oaths that the swearer has no intention of keeping
	reprevable blameworthy
348	**Witnesse on Mathew** [See Matthew, chapter 5 verses 33-34.]
349	**Jeremye** [See Jeremiah, chapter 4 verse 2.]
350	**sooth** truthfully
351	**And swere ... rightwisnesse** and swear in judgment and also in righteousness [i.e. in court when a solemn oath is demanded]

The follies of gambling, particularly among rulers, is exposed. The Pardoner moves on to oath-taking, citing the Bible as authority for condemning false or habitual oaths. He urges that oaths should be few, and taken only when really necessary, as in court. He then begins to deal with idle oaths, taking the name of God in vain.

For which, as soone as it mighte be,
He stal him hoom again to his contree,
And seyde, 'Ther wol I nat lese my name,   325
Ne I wol nat take on me so greet defame,
Yow for to allie unto none hasardours.
Sendeth othere wise embassadours;
For, by my trouthe, me were levere die
Than I yow sholde to hasardours allye.   330
For ye, that been so glorious in honours,
Shul nat allyen yow with hasardours
As by my wil, ne as by my tretee.'
This wise philosophre, thus seyde hee.
    Looke eek that to the king Demetrius,   335
The king of Parthes, as the book seith us,
Sente him a paire of dees of gold in scorn,
For he hadde used hasard ther-biforn;
For which he heeld his glorie or his renoun
At no value or reputacioun.   340
Lordes may finden oother maner pley
Honest ynough to drive the day awey.
    Now wol I speke of othes false and grete
A word or two, as olde bookes trete.
Gret swering is a thing abhominable,   345
And fals swering is yet moore reprevable.
The heighe God forbad swering at al,
Witnesse on Mathew; but in special
Of swering seith the hooly Jeremye,
'Thou shalt swere sooth thine othes, and nat lie,   350
And swere in doom, and eek in rightwisnesse';
But idel swering is a cursednesse.

In line 375 The Pardoner returns quite suddenly to his narrative which he left equally suddenly at line 191.

There is mention in line 376 of prime, the first of the day's services in a monastery. There were seven of these services, known as canonical hours. Prime began early, at about 6 a.m.

- Can you see – or hear – any changes in the language and verse at line 375? You might examine the punctuation before this line and after it.
- Read lines 375-83 again. What impressions of action and feeling do you receive?
- In what ways do you think Chaucer has brought together in these lines the various sins that have been listed so far?

353 **firste table** first tablet [i.e. of the Ten Commandments brought down by Moses from Mount Sinai. This one would have contained the first five commandments.]

354 **heestes** commandments

356 **amis** wrongly, in vain [amiss]

357-8 **Lo, rather ... thing** see, he forbids such swearing before murder or many a damnable thing [This second commandment comes before the commandment against killing, and could therefore be seen as more important.]

359 **as by ordre** [i.e. the order of the Ten Commandments]

360 **This knoweth ... understondeth** anyone knows this who understands his commandments

362 **al plat** flatly

363-4 **That vengeance ... outrageous** [God's] vengeance shall not leave the house of him who is too excessive in his oaths

366 **Hayles** [an abbey in Gloucestershire that possessed what was thought to be a small glass bottle of Christ's blood]

367 **chaunce** [a throw of the dice in the game called Hasard which neither wins or loses; it entitles the player to a second turn]

cynk and treye five and three [French numbers were used in card games, as they sometimes are today.]

370 **bicched bones** cursed dice [carved from bone]

371 **forswering, ire** breaking one's word, anger

373 **lete** avoid, give up

376 **Longe erst ... belle** long before any bell for prime was rung [There is a suggestion here that in the inverted world of these rioters – who worshipped the devil (see line 184) – the day started even earlier than the hour for prime.].

379 **Biforn ... grave** before [in front of] a corpse as it was being carried to its grave

380 **knave** serving boy

381 **bet** quickly [*literally:* 'better']

axe redily ask quickly

The Pardoner returns to Christianity, quoting the Ten Commandments as his authority for attacking the various sins. He returns abruptly to his tale.

Bihoold and se that in the firste table
Of heighe Goddes heestes honurable,
Hou that the seconde heeste of him is this: 355
'Take nat my name in idel or amis.'
Lo, rather he forbedeth swich swering
Than homicide or many a cursed thing;
I seye that, as by ordre, thus it stondeth;
This knoweth, that his heestes understondeth,   360
How that the seconde heeste of God is that.
And forther over, I wol thee telle al plat,
That vengeance shal nat parten from his hous
That of his othes is to outrageous.
'By Goddes precious herte,' and 'By his nailes,'   365
 And 'By the blood of Crist that is in Hayles,
Sevene is my chaunce, and thyn is cynk and treye!'
'By Goddes armes, if thou falsly pleye,
This daggere shal thurghout thyn herte go!'—
This fruit cometh of the bicched bones two,   370
Forswering, ire, falsnesse, homicide.
Now, for the love of Crist, that for us dyde,
Lete youre othes, bothe grete and smale.
But, sires, now wol I telle forth my tale.
   Thise riotoures thre of whiche I telle,   375
Longe erst er prime rong of any belle,
Were set hem in a taverne for to drinke,
And as they sat, they herde a belle clinke
Biforn a cors, was caried to his grave.
That oon of hem gan callen to his knave: 380
'Go bet,' quod he, 'and axe redily
What cors is this that passeth heer forby;
And looke that thou reporte his name weel.'

- Read lines 383-98 aloud. The rioters receive a warning about Death. Write a paragraph explaining in detail your impression of these lines.
- 'The child seith sooth' (line 400). Write a paragraph explaining exactly what the 'taverner' understands by the child's warning. Consider also why he might have interpreted the remark in this way.
- What impression do you receive from the oaths involving parts of God's body and the figure of death? What does this tell you about blasphemy?
- Practise reading this page aloud in a small group, so as to bring out the language and attitudes of the four characters.

384	**never-a-deel** not at all	398	**dame** mother
385	**er ye cam heer two houres** two hours before you arrived here	401	**henne over a mile** over a mile from here
387	**to-night** during the night, or perhaps last night		**greet** great, big
		402	**hine** labourer
388	**fordronke** completely drunk	404	**To been ... were** it would be very wise to be careful
389	**privee** stealthy		
	clepeth call	407	**swich** such
390	**sleeth** kills [slayeth]	408	**by wey and eek by strete** in every road and also every street
391	**And with his spere** [Death is personified and has a spear with which to kill people.]	409	**I make ... bones** I swear by God's noble bones [a drunken oath and a reminder of the 'bicched bones' at line 370]
393	**pestilence** outbreak of plague		
397	**beth redy** be [plural] ready		
	everemoore always		

'Ther cam a privee theef man clepeth Deeth,
That in this contree al the peple sleeth'

The serving boy knows exactly what happened, and gives a graphic account of the activities of Death. With great oaths the drunken rioter determines to seek out this Death and kill him. He calls upon his friends to swear a mighty oath to do away with Death that very day.

'Sire,' quod this boy, 'it nedeth never-a-deel;
It was me toold er ye cam heer two houres.   385
He was, pardee, an old felawe of youres;
And sodeynly he was yslain to-night,
Fordronke, as he sat on his bench upright.
Ther cam a privee theef man clepeth Deeth,
That in this contree al the peple sleeth,   390
And with his spere he smoot his herte atwo,
And wente his wey withouten wordes mo.
He hath a thousand slain this pestilence.
And, maister, a ye come in his presence,
Me thinketh that it were necessarie   395
For to be war of swich an adversarie.
Beth redy for to meete him everemoore;
Thus taughte me my dame; I sey namoore.'
'By seinte Marie,' seyde this taverner,
'The child seith sooth, for he hath slain this yeer,   400
Henne over a mile, withinne a greet village,
Bothe man and womman, child, and hine, and page;
I trowe his habitacioun be there.
To been avised greet wisdom it were,
Er that he dide a man a dishonour.'   405
    'Ye, Goddes armes!' quod this riotour,
'Is it swich peril with him for to meete?
I shal him seke by wey and eek by strete,
I make avow to Goddes digne bones!
Herkneth, felawes, we thre been al ones;   410
Lat ech of us holde up his hand til oother,
And ech of us bicomen otheres brother,
And we wol sleen this false traitour Deeth.
He shal be slain, he that so manye sleeth,
By Goddes dignitee, er it be night.'   415

- To what extent would you say the vocabulary, tone, and movement of the verse in lines 416-24 echo the drunken actions described?
- Write a paragraph describing in detail the old man's attitude to old age and death, and contrast it with that of the three rioters.
- Practise reading these lines aloud in a small group, dramatising them so as to bring out the language and attitudes of the four characters.

416   **togidres** together

      hir trouthes plight swore their solemn oath

418   **ybore** natural

423   **And Cristes blessed body al torente** [Compare with lines 188-89.]

424   **hente** catch

426   **Right as they ... stile** just as they were about to climb over a stile

429   **God yow see!** may God look after you

431   **carl** man

with sory grace [a vague phrase that might mean 'you ugly old fool' or 'bad luck to you']

432   **forwrapped** completely wrapped [See also 'fordronke' line 388.]

433   **livestow** do you live [livest thou]

434   **visage** face

436   **though that I walked into Inde** though I walked to India [i.e. to the ends of the earth]

439   **moot I han myn age stille** I must continue to keep my age

The oath taken, the three drunken men stagger off towards the village where Death was reported to be. On the way they meet an old man, muffled in his cloak, and scornfully ask him why he bothers to go on living. He tells them that he cannot find anyone willing to exchange their youth for his age: not even Death wants his life.

Togidres han thise thre hir trouthes plight
To live and dien ech of hem for oother,
As though he were his owene ybore brother.
And up they stirte, al dronken in this rage,
And forth they goon towardes that village   420
Of which the taverner hadde spoke biforn.
And many a grisly ooth thanne han they sworn,
And Cristes blessed body al torente—
Deeth shal be deed, if that they may him hente.
Whan they han goon nat fully half a mile,   425
Right as they wolde han troden over a stile,
An oold man and a povre with hem mette.
This olde man ful mekely hem grette,
And seyde thus, 'Now, lordes, God yow see!'
The proudeste of thise riotoures three   430
Answerde again, 'What, carl, with sory grace!
Why artow al forwrapped save thy face?
Why livestow so longe in so greet age?'
This olde man gan looke in his visage,
And seyde thus: 'For I ne kan nat finde   435
A man, though that I walked into Inde,
Neither in citee ne in no village,
That wolde chaunge his youthe for myn age;
And therfore moot I han myn age stille,
As longe time as it is Goddes wille.   440
Ne Deeth, allas, ne wol nat han my lyf.

A tradition in painting grew up in the years following the Black Death of a personified Death taking away the young, the rich and the beautiful, but leaving the old and poor. The pictures show the latter stretching out their hands to Death, as if beseeching to be taken instead. The Black Death apparently took more young than old people.

- Write a paragraph describing the old man's experience of life at his age.
- List the useful injunctions the old man makes to the rioters about their behaviour to him and about their way of life.
- Look again at lines 471-3. In what ways might this be a further development of the rioters' blasphemy? You might bear in mind the strange nature of the old man and the reasons the rioters might have for accusing him of being Death's spy.
- How far do you think the words of the old man add to the warnings the rioters have already received in lines 375-98?

442   **kaitif** wretch

443   **moodres** mother's

445   **leeve mooder** dear mother [i.e. the earth]

446   **vanisshe** wither, languish

448-50   **Mooder ... wrappe in me** [The old man tells the earth, his mother, that he wants to exchange his chest full of clothes for a single garment.]

an heyre clowt a haircloth shroud

451   **grace** favour

452   **welked** withered

453   **to yow** in you [Lines 453-4 contain a conventional antithesis often found in medieval literature – gross rudeness contrasted with courtly politeness.]

455   **but** unless

457   **Agains** in the company of

hoor upon his heed white-haired [a suggestion of frost upon his head]

458   **reed** advise [The quotation in lines 457-8 is from Leviticus, chapter 19 verse 32.]

461   **In age ... abide** in old age, if you live so long

462   **where ye go or ride** whether you walk or ride

463   **thider** thither, there [The old man's destination is unknown – part of the mystery surrounding him.]

465   **hasardour** gambler [By now the gambling is beginning to be a gamble with life and death.]

469   **espye** spy

470   **abye** pay for

471   **the hooly sacrement** [i.e. the sacrament of communion, hence God's body]

472   **oon of his assent** in agreement with him, in league with him

The old man paints an eerie picture of knocking on the ground, seeking entry to the earth, his mother, so that he can rest in the grave. He remonstrates with the rioters for their lack of courtesy, reminding them of the injunctions in the Bible to treat old people with respect. He is about to leave, but the rioters detain him as Death's spy, with a rough and blasphemous demand for Death's whereabouts.

Thus walke I, lyk a restelees kaitif,
And on the ground, which is my moodres gate,
I knokke with my staf, bothe erly and late,
And seye, "Leeve mooder, leet me in!   445
Lo how I vanisshe, flessh and blood and skin!
Allas! whan shul my bones been at reste?
Mooder, with yow wolde I chaunge my cheste
That in my chambre longe time hath be,
Ye, for an heyre clowt to wrappe in me."   450
But yet to me she wol nat do that grace,
For which ful pale and welked is my face.
   But sires, to yow it is no curteisye
To speken to an old man vileynye,
But he trespasse in word, or elles in dede.   455
In Hooly Writ ye may yourself wel rede:
"Agains an oold man, hoor upon his heed,
Ye sholde arise;" wherfore I yeve yow reed,
Ne dooth unto an oold man noon harm now,
Namoore than that ye wolde men did to yow   460
In age, if that ye so longe abide.
And God be with yow, where ye go or ride!
I moot go thider as I have to go.'
   'Nay, olde cherl, by God, thou shalt nat so,'
Seyde this oother hasardour anon;   465
'Thou partest nat so lightly, by Seint John!
Thou spak right now of thilke traitour Deeth,
That in this contree alle oure freendes sleeth.
Have heer my trouthe, as thou art his espye,
Telle where he is, or thou shalt it abye,   470
By God, and by the hooly sacrement!
For soothly thou art oon of his assent
To sleen us yonge folk, thou false theef!'

- What warnings does the old man give the rioters here? Look carefully at the detail of lines 474-81.
- What do you think the character of the old man might represent or suggest, beyond the literal view of him taken by the rioters?
- The rioters are looking for Death and have found enormous quantities of gold beneath a tree. What in your view is Chaucer suggesting here, bearing in mind that they are serving the devil, and are looking for death rather than life?
- Define, briefly but as exactly as you can, the meaning of 'felicitee' in line 501.
- On what grounds do you think the 'worste of hem' in lines 493, 500 and 504, declares the treasure to be theirs?

474 **be so leef** if you would so much like

476 **by my fey** by my faith

478 **youre boost** your boast [that they will kill Death] will in no way make him hide

479 **ook** oak

480-1 **God save yow ... amende** may God the saviour of mankind redeem you and make you better

484 **florins** gold coins [so called from Florence, the banking capital of Europe]

485 **busshels** [A bushel was a large dry measure of volume. This quantity of gold coins was clearly a fantastic amount.]

as hem thoughte as it seemed to them [A suggestion that they were being deceived, or were deceiving themselves?]

492 **My wit ... pleye** my intelligence is great, although I joke and play

493-5 **This tresor ... spende** [Compare these lines with lines 8-10.]

496 **who wende** who would have thought

497 **grace** stroke of luck [Compare with line 451.]

500 **woot** know

501 **felicitee** happiness [particularly in the sense of complete or heavenly happiness. The word can mean also blessedness; its meaning varies throughout the tales according to context and the understanding of the character that utters it.]

502 **trewely** truly [another word with similar variations in meaning]

503 **stronge** blatant

504 **doon us honge** hang us

The old man tells them where to find Death and calls on God to protect them. They run and find a huge hoard of gold under an oak tree, and immediately begin to plan their future lives. They start to think how they might move the gold, by night, to their own houses.

'Now, sires,' quod he, 'if that yow be so leef
To finde Deeth, turne up this croked wey,   475
For in that grove I lafte him, by my fey,
Under a tree, and there he wole abide;
Noght for youre boost he wole him no thing hide.
Se ye that ook? Right there ye shal him finde.
God save yow, that boghte again mankinde,   480
And yow amende.' Thus seyde this olde man;
And everich of thise riotoures ran
Til he cam to that tree, and ther they founde
Of florins fine of gold ycoined rounde
Wel ny an eighte busshels, as hem thoughte.   485
No lenger thanne after Deeth they soughte,
But ech of hem so glad was of that sighte,
For that the florins been so faire and brighte,
That doun they sette hem by this precious hoord.
The worste of hem, he spak the firste word.   490
    'Bretheren,' quod he, 'taak kep what that I seye;
My wit is greet, though that I bourde and pleye.
This tresor hath Fortune unto us yiven,
In mirthe and joliftee oure lyf to liven,
And lightly as it comth, so wol we spende.   495
Ey! Goddes precious dignitee! who wende
To-day that we sholde han so fair a grace?
But mighte this gold be caried fro this place
Hoom to myn hous—or elles unto youres
(For wel ye woot that al this gold is oures)—   500
Thanne were we in heigh felicitee.
But trewely, by daye it may nat bee.
Men wolde seyn that we were theves stronge,
And for oure owene tresor doon us honge.

'Se ye that ook? Right there ye shal him finde'

- Read St John's Gospel, chapter 19, verses 17-34, then re-read lines 474-519. What echoes of the Gospel do you think the pilgrims might hear in these lines? What echoes might the Pardoner hear?
- Examine the logic of the rioter's statement and question in lines 522-9. Write a paragraph explaining your view of this statement, bearing in mind the earlier statements the three rioters have made to each other.

506	**As wisely ... mighte** as cleverly and as secretly as possible		**tarie** delay
507-8	**cut among us alle/ Be drawe** that we all draw lots [with lengths of cut straw]	515	**by oon assent** by agreement
		516	**fest** fist
		522	**sworen** true [See line 418.]
509	**herte blithe** with a joyful heart	526	**departed** divided
510	**renne** run	527	**shape it** arrange it
	swithe quickly	529	**torn** turn
511	**breed and wyn** [Note the suggestion of Holy Communion.]	530	**I noot** I do not know [*literally:* I know not]
512	**subtilly** cleverly	533	**conseil** secret
513	**wol** does		**shrewe** villain

As the treasure can only be moved by night, the ringleader suggests that one of them should run to the town for bread and wine while the other two remain on guard. They draw lots and the youngest goes away. The first rioter then suggests to his companion that he knows a way of dividing the treasure two ways instead of three, and if the other agrees to join him in conspiracy, will tell him how it could be done.

This tresor moste ycaried be by nighte   505
As wisely and as slyly as it mighte.
Wherfore I rede that cut among us alle
Be drawe, and lat se wher the cut wol falle;
And he that hath the cut with herte blithe
Shal renne to the town, and that ful swithe,   510
And bringe us breed and wyn ful prively.
And two of us shul kepen subtilly
This tresor wel; and if he wol nat tarie,
Whan it is night, we wol this tresor carie,
By oon assent, where as us thinketh best.'   515
That oon of hem the cut broghte in his fest,
And bad hem drawe, and looke where it wol falle;
And it fil on the yongeste of hem alle,
And forth toward the toun he wente anon.
And also soone as that he was gon,   520
That oon of hem spak thus unto that oother:
'Thow knowest wel thou art my sworen brother;
Thy profit wol I telle thee anon.
Thou woost wel that oure felawe is agon.
And heere is gold, and that ful greet plentee,   525
That shal departed been among us thre.
But nathelees, if I kan shape it so
That it departed were among us two,
Hadde I nat doon a freendes torn to thee?'
     That oother answerde, 'I noot how that may be.   530
He woot wel that the gold is with us tweye;
What shal we doon? What shal we to him seye?'
     'Shal it be conseil?' seyde the firste shrewe,
'And I shal tellen in a wordes fewe
What we shal doon, and bringe it wel aboute.'   535

53

- What evidence of loyalty among thieves can you see in lines 536-48?
- What tone do you think would have to be adopted to recite line 546?
- Read aloud lines 538-48 and lines 554-7. Contrast the manner and style of speech in these lines with other statements made by the rioters earlier in the text.
- What view of the life of a rich man do the rioters have?

536-7   **'I graunte ... biwreye'** 'I agree completely,' said the other, 'that I will keep my oath and not betray you.'

539   **strenger** stronger

540   **whan that he is set** when he has sat down

542   **rive** split

544   **looke thou do the same** make sure you do the same

546   **bitwixen** between

547   **oure lustes all fulfille** satisfy all our desires

548   **at oure owene wille** as much as we want to

550   **thridde** third

554   **if so were that** if it were to happen that

556   **trone** throne

557   **murye** happily

558   **feend** fiend, devil

559   **beye** buy

561-2   **For why ... bringe** because the devil found him in such a state he was allowed (by God) to bring him to sorrow [The suggestion is that his soul, full of murderous thoughts, was ripe for the devil's purposes. There is a hint here of the Pardoner's sermon.]

563   **For this ... entente** for this was utterly his [the rioter's] complete intention

*'And forth he gooth, no lenger wolde he tarie
Into the toun, unto a pothecarie'*

Having promised loyalty, the rioter receives his instructions for the murder. He finds that he must incriminate himself thoroughly by stabbing his victim while pretending to wrestle with him playfully. Neither plotter is aware of the grim determination of their young victim to poison them both and enjoy all the gold – and to then be the merriest man under God's throne.

'I graunte,' quod that oother, 'out of doute,
That, by my trouthe, I wol thee nat biwreye.'
'Now,' quod the firste, 'thou woost wel we be tweye,
And two of us shul strenger be than oon.
Looke whan that he is set, that right anoon   540
Aris as though thou woldest with him pleye,
And I shal rive him thurgh the sides tweye
Whil that thou strogelest with him as in game,
And with thy daggere looke thou do the same;
And thanne shal al this gold departed be,   545
My deere freend, bitwixen me and thee.
Thanne may we bothe oure lustes all fulfille,
And pleye at dees right at oure owene wille.'
And thus acorded been thise shrewes tweye
To sleen the thridde, as ye han herd me seye.   550
   This yongeste, which that wente to the toun,
Ful ofte in herte he rolleth up and doun
The beautee of thise florins newe and brighte.
'O Lord!' quod he, 'if so were that I mighte
Have al this tresor to myself allone,   555
Ther is no man that liveth under the trone
Of God that sholde live so murye as I.'
And atte laste the feend, oure enemy,
Putte in his thought that he sholde poison beye,
With which he mighte sleen his felawes tweye;   560
For-why the feend foond him in swich livinge
That he hadde leve him to sorwe bringe.
For this was outrely his fulle entente,
To sleen hem bothe, and nevere to repente.

- The young rioter has no difficulty in getting the poison. Look back at lines 561-4 and write a paragraph about the meaning of this passage as it might have been understood by the Pardoner's listeners.
- The action is speeding up, and the young rioter runs 'into the nexte strete'. How would you describe the significance of this action in the light of what he has just been told in lines 579-81?
- Look back over the Tale, note those places where swift action occurs, and write an account of the possible moral and spiritual significance of these moments.
- Write a paragraph explaining the irony of the apothecary's earnest assurance on line 574.
- Read lines 565-581 aloud in a small group, trying as far as possible to bring out the thoughts that might lie behind the words.

565	**tarie** stay, delay		578	**forlete** lose
566	**pothecarie** apothecary, pharmacist		579	**in lasse while** in less time
568	**quelle** kill		580	**goon a paas** walk at an normal pace
569	**hawe** yard		582	**yhent** took, grasped
570	**capouns** chickens		583	**sith** then
571	**wreke** revenge		585	**botelles** bottles
576	**confiture** concoction		587	**thridde** third
577	**Noght but the ... whete** no more than the amount of a grain of wheat			

The young rioter buys poison immediately. The apothecary promises, on his hope of salvation, that nothing can long survive his best poison. The rioter rushes off with it to borrow three bottles, into two of which he puts the poison.

And forth he gooth, no lenger wolde he tarie,   565
Into the toun, unto a pothecarie,
And preyde him that he him wolde selle
Som poison, that he mighte his rattes quelle;
And eek ther was a polcat in his hawe,
That, as he seyde, his capouns hadde yslawe,   570
And fain he wolde wreke him, if he mighte,
On vermin that destroyed him by nighte.
   The pothecarie answerde, 'And thou shalt have
A thing that, also God my soule save,
In al this world ther is no creature,   575
That eten or dronken hath of this confiture
Noght but the montance of a corn of whete,
That he ne shal his lif anon forlete;
Ye, sterve he shal, and that in lasse while
Than thou wolt goon a paas nat but a mile,   580
This poisoun is so strong and violent.'
   This cursed man hath in his hond yhent
This poisoun in a box, and sith he ran
Into the nexte strete unto a man,
And borwed of him large botelles thre;   585
And in the two his poison poured he;
The thridde he kepte clene for his drinke.

In lines 609-17 the Pardoner ends his story with a conventional exclamation, under-lining the gravity of the sin of blasphemy, to which all the other sins listed have led the rioters.

- Who do you think the Pardoner means when he says in line 612 'Thou blasphemour'?
- Read lines 597-8 aloud. What effect do you think they have in the context in which they occur?
- What significance do you think the Pardoner's listeners might attach to the fact that the remaining rioters are killed when one gives the other wine to drink?
- Read lines 614-17. What effect do you think is achieved by placing 'mankinde' at the beginning of the sentence and 'unkinde' at the end?
- Practise reading aloud lines 593-617 while others mime the action so as to suggest the deceit and the murderous intentions of all three characters.

588	**shoop him for to swinke** he planned to labour		**fen** section [i.e. in any section or sub-division of his writings]
590	**with sorry grace** accursed	605	**mo wonder** more wondrous
592	**repaireth** returns	606	**er hir ending** before they died
593	**sermone of it** talk about it	607	**homicides** murderers
594	**cast** planned	610	**homicide** homicidal, murderous
599	**par cas** by chance	613	**grete** great
602	**storven** died [past tense of 'starve']		**usage** habit
603	**Avycen** Avicen [a great Arab philoso-pher and physician]	614	**bitide** happen
604	**wroot** wrote	615	**That to ... wroghte** that to thy creator, who made you
	canon rule [One of Avicen's most influential works was entitled *The Book of the Canon in Medicine*, an influential text book for many years.]	616	**And with his ... boghte** and with his precious heart's blood redeemed you
		617	**unkinde** unnatural

The youngest rioter shows himself to be equally effective in plotting his own gain. However, when he returns to the others he is swiftly killed. His killers celebrate with the bottles of wine he has provided, and die a horrible death from the poison. The Pardoner proclaims the vileness of the sins that led to this event.

For al the night he shoop him for to swinke
In caryinge of the gold out of that place.
And whan this riotour, with sory grace,   590
Hadde filled with wyn his grete botels thre,
To his felawes again repaireth he.
    What nedeth it to sermone of it moore?
For right as they hadde cast his deeth bifoore,
Right so they han him slain, and that anon.   595
And whan that this was doon, thus spak that oon:
'Now lat us sitte and drinke, and make us merie,
    And afterward we wol his body berie.'
And with that word it happed him, par cas,
To take the botel ther the poison was,   600
And drank, and yaf his felawe drinke also,
For which anon they storven bothe two.
    But certes, I suppose that Avycen
Wroot nevere in no canon, ne in no fen,
Mo wonder signes of empoisoning   605
Than hadde thise wrecches two, er hir ending.
Thus ended been thise homicides two,
And eek the false empoisonere also.
    O cursed sinne of alle cursednesse!
O traitours homicide, O wikkednesse!   610
O glotonye, luxurie, and hasardrye!
Thou blasphemour of Crist with vileynye
And othes grete, of usage and of pride!
Allas! mankinde, how may it bitide
That to thy creatour, which that the wroghte,   615
And with his precious herte-blood thee boghte,
Thou art so fals and so unkinde, allas?

The Pardoner's demands for cash or valuables in exchange for the forgiveness of sins represents one of the worst abuses of the doctrine of indulgences; it entirely leaves out the matter of repentance and contrition. The Pardoner is not a priest and cannot therefore hear confessions. In effect he is saying that buying his pardon is the equivalent of confession, repentance, absolution and penance.

- Write a paragraph explaining in detail the change of tone that happens at this point in the tale.
- To what extent do you think the Pardoner is aware of how others might see him at this point of his discourse, bearing in mind that he has made no secret of his motivation?

618 **foryeve yow youre trespas** forgive you your sins

619 **ware yow fro** and lead you from

620 **warice** heed, take heed of

621 **so that** as long as [See also line 643.]

nobles coins worth one third of one pound

sterlinges pennies

623 **Boweth youre heed** bow [plural imperative] your heads

623 **bulle** licence, official church document

624 **wives** women

wolle wool

625 **rolle** list [i.e. of those whose sins he claimed to have removed, and who could therefore enter heaven]

627 **assoille** absolve [you of your sins]

628 **Yow that wol offre** you who wish to make an offering

630 **leche** leech [i.e. doctor]

634 **male** bag

636 **yeven** given

637 **of devocion** out of devotion [to God]

641 **wende** go, travel

643 **So that ... newe** as long as you make a fresh offering every time

644 **whiche that be goode and trewe** [pence] that are the real thing [i.e. not counterfeit]

645 **everich** everyone

646 **mowe** may

suffisant sufficient [i.e. licensed]

647 **in contree as ye ride** as you ride through the country

648 **For aventures** in case of accidents

bitide happen

'So that ye offre nobles or sterlinges,
Or elles silver broches, spoones, ringes'

The Pardoner switches abruptly into his sales pitch. He reminds his congregation to avoid the sin of avarice by providing money and goods in payment for his pardons. Equally abruptly he ends his sample sermon and addresses his fellow pilgrims directly, reminding them that he has relics and pardons for sale. He tells them that they are honoured to travel in the company of a pardoner, who, continually refreshed with money, can continually pardon them their sins.

Now, goode men, God foryeve yow youre trespas,
And ware yow fro the sinne of avarice!
Myn hooly pardoun may yow alle warice,   620
So that ye offre nobles or sterlinges,
Or elles silver broches, spoones, ringes.
Boweth youre heed under this hooly bulle!
Cometh up, ye wives, offreth of youre wolle!
Youre names I entre heer in my rolle anon;   625
Into the blisse of hevene shul ye gon.
I yow assoille by myn heigh power,
Yow that wol offre, as clene and eek as cleer
As ye were born.—And lo, sires, thus I preche.
And Jhesu Crist, that is oure soules leche,   630
So graunte yow his pardoun to receive,
For that is best; I wol yow nat deceive.
    But sires, o word forgat I in my tale:
I have relikes and pardoun in my male
As faire as any man in Engelond,   635
Whiche were me yeven by the popes hond.
If any of yow wole, of devocion,
Offren, and han myn absolucion,
Com forth anon, and kneleth heere adoun,
And mekely receiveth my pardoun;   640
Or elles taketh pardoun as ye wende,
Al newe and fressh at every miles ende,
So that ye offren, alwey newe and newe,
Nobles or pens, whiche that be goode and trewe.
It is an honour to everich that is heer   645
That ye mowe have a suffisant pardoneer
T'assoille yow, in contree as ye ride,
For aventures whiche that may bitide.

- Given that the Pardoner has been drinking, and therefore perhaps most in danger of falling from his horse, and that he is himself in need of absolution, what can you say about his understanding of religion?
- On the evidence of these lines, to what extent do you think the Pardoner has misjudged his audience?
- The Host makes two references to religion in these lines. Is either of these statements blasphemous, and if so, why?
- How far would you say that the Host has, in his anger, made an effective response to the content of the Pardoner's Prologue and Tale?
- Look back to the description of the Pardoner from the General Prologue (page 13). Do you think the suggestions of his ambiguous sexuality have any symbolic significance in the light of the way of life he leads?

649	**paraventure** perhaps	662	**breech** underpants
650	**atwo** in two	664	**with thy fundement depeint** stained with your bum
651	**seuretee** security		
652	**That I am ...yfalle** that I should happen to be in your company	665	**by the crois which that Seint Eleyne fond** [Saint Helen, mother of the Emperor Constantine, was tradition- ally the finder of the remains of Christ's cross.]
653	**moore and lasse** high and low [in rank]		
655	**rede** suggest		
658	**everychon** every one	666	**coillons** balls
659	**grote** groat [coin worth perhaps £20 in today's money]	667	**seintuarie** reliquary [box, usually decorated, for keeping and displaying relics]
	unbokele unfasten, unbuckle		
660	**thanne have I Cristes curs** I would have the curse of Christ if I were to do that	668	**Lat kutte ... carie** let them be cut off [and] I will help you carry them
661	**so theech** so may I prosper	669	**They shul ... toord** they shall be enshrined in a pig's turd [for a reliquary]

The Pardoner repeats his call to his listeners to pay up and receive pardon, telling the Host he is the most in need. This provokes a splendidly vulgar outburst from the Host, suggesting that the Pardoner would sell his dirty pants as a relic. He tells the Pardoner that he would like to castrate him and enshrine his testicles in the most disgusting object he can think of.

Paraventure ther may fallen oon or two
Doun of his hors, and breke his nekke atwo.   650
Looke which a seuretee is it to yow alle
That I am in youre felaweshipe yfalle,
That may assoille yow, bothe moore and lasse,
Whan that the soule shal fro the body passe.
I rede that oure Hoost heere shal biginne,   655
For he is moost envoluped in sinne.
Com forth, sire Hoost, and offre first anon,
And thou shalt kisse the relikes everychon,
Ye, for a grote! Unbokele anon thy purs.
    'Nay, nay,' quod he, 'thanne have I Cristes curs!   660
Lat be,' quod he, 'it shal nat be, so theech!
Thou woldest make me kisse thyn olde breech,
And swere it were a relik of a seint,
Though it were with thy fundement depeint!
But, by the crois which that Seint Eleyne fond   665
I wolde I hadde thy coillons in myn hond
In stide of relikes or of seintuarie.
Lat kutte hem of, I wol thee helpe hem carie;
They shul be shrined in an hogges toord!'

- How far, and in what ways, would you say that the influence of the traditional social and religious order is seen in these lines? Bear in mind the depth of feelings that the Pardoner must have provoked throughout his Prologue and Tale.

671   **wrooth** angry

672   **pleye** [i.e. play the game of exchanging tales on the pilgrimage]

675   **lough** laughed

676   **it is right ynough** that is enough

677   **myrie** merry, happy

      cheere mood

679   **yow** the respectful plural form of 'you' [equivalent to the modern French 'vous'. The Knight is being gracious or 'gentil', as befits his rank and way of life.]

680   **thee** the familiar singular form of 'you' [equivalent to the modern French 'tu'. The Knight appears to be drawing a moral distinction between the Host and the Pardoner.]

681   **as we diden** as we were doing [before this incident]

There is a sulphurous anger between the Pardoner and the Host, who feels that the whole
enterprise of the pilgrimage is threatened, but the Knight intervenes and restores harmony.

This Pardoner answerde nat a word;   670
So wrooth he was, no word ne wolde he seye.
   'Now,' quod oure Hoost, 'I wol no lenger pleye
With thee, ne with noon oother angry man.'
But right anon the worthy Knight bigan,
Whan that he saugh that al the peple lough,   675
'Namoore of this, for it is right ynough.
Sire Pardoner, be glad and myrie of cheere;
And ye, sire Hoost, that been to me so deere,
I prey yow that ye kisse the Pardoner.
And Pardoner, I prey thee, drawe thee neer,   680
And, as we diden, lat us laughe and pleye.'
Anon they kiste, and riden forth hir weye.

The tale told by the Pardoner

Like many stories in late medieval and early modern literature, the tale told by the Pardoner is not original. There are many versions of the basic story of three men who stumble across great wealth, ignore warnings – usually from an old man – that it will be the death of them, and then plot to kill each other in the hope of enjoying the wealth by themselves. Even the stabbing and the poisoning are common details in a number of versions of this moral tale. Originality in literature, in the sense that we now value it, did not concern Chaucer or his readers.

Chaucer did make this story his own, however, by his treatment of it. The mysterious nature and quality of the old man is entirely his, for instance. So too is the structure, with the tale abandoned almost at the outset while the Pardoner gives an astonishing demonstration of the power of his preaching before returning to his narrative. The context of the Prologue and Tale is unique to Chaucer: the various statements by the Host provide a dramatic framework for the Pardoner's contribution to the entertainment of the pilgrims; and further significance is provided by the description of the Pardoner in the General Prologue. The Pardoner is one among many pilgrims on the road to Canterbury, and his account is part of a larger story.

The impact of Chaucer's version of the story is greatly increased by the impassioned sermon on gluttony that interrupts it. The story proper does not get under way until we have been told, in the sermon (and by the manner in which the sermon is delivered) what is wrong with the lives of the rioters in the story. We find new layers of meaning at every stage, even at the end of the Tale, when the ugliness of the Host's anger at the Pardoner's insulting attempt to defraud him is overcome by the insistence of the Knight that they accord each other Christian forgiveness. It is ironic that the appalling Pardoner, who is thought by the Host to be able to offer no more than some crudity to amuse the party, tells one of the most clearly moral tales in the whole of *The Canterbury Tales*.

The sequence may be summarised as follows:
- the Pardoner's dreadful character is introduced in the General Prologue
- the Physician tells a tale – rather poorly – with an unconvincing recommendation of honesty
- the Host tells the Pardoner to tell them 'some moral thing', which he has to think hard about
- the Pardoner starts his Prologue with a shockingly honest account of his motives and actions
- he starts his Tale, which is to be an attack on the vices of which he has accused himself
- he breaks off his Tale to give a sample of his methods and performance in the pulpit
- he returns to his Tale and tells it with great power
- he abruptly – and 'honestly' – sets out to sell his relics and pardons to the pilgrims
- the Host condemns him but is persuaded to make peace by the Knight.

Chaucer's pilgrims

The Canterbury pilgrims leaving the Tabard Inn at Southwark

In order of appearance:

The Knight	brave, devout and unassuming – the perfect gentleman
The Squire	in training to follow in the Knight, his father's, footsteps, a fine and fashionable young man, and madly in love
The Yeoman	the Knight's only servant, a skilled bowman and forester
The Prioress	a most ladylike head of a nunnery; she takes great pains with her appearance and manners; she loves animals. She is accompanied by another nun and three priests, the nun and one priest also telling tales
The Monk	fine and prosperous looking, well-mounted; he loves hunting
The Friar	cheerful and sociable, he is skilled at obtaining alms from those he visits, particularly the ladies
The Merchant	rather secretive; his main interest is commerce
The Clerk	thin and shabby, his passion is scholarship; he spends all he has on books
The Sergeant at Law	a judge at the assize courts; skilled at making personal profit from his office; one of the few pilgrims about whom Chaucer says very little
The Franklin	a wealthy and hospitable landowner and a JP; but not a member of the aristocracy
The Five Guildsmen	although they pursue different crafts or trades, they belong to the same social guild – rather self-important townsfolk
The Cook	he has been brought along to provide meals for the guildsmen; although he is a versatile cook, Chaucer suggests his personal hygiene could be improved

The Shipman	a weather-beaten master mariner and pirate
The Doctor of Physic	finely dressed and a skilled medical practitioner; he is an expert in astrology and natural magic; he loves gold
The Wife of Bath	skilled at weaving; her chief claim to fame is her five husbands
The Parson	the only truly devout churchman in Chaucer's group; he avoids all the tricks unscrupulous clerics used to get rich, and spends his care and energy on his parishioners
The Ploughman	the Parson's brother and, like him, a simple, honest hardworking man
The Miller	tough, ugly and a cheat
The Manciple	responsible for organising the provisions for the lawyers in one of the Inns of Court – a plum job for a clever man
The Reeve	unsociable, but able; the estate manager of a young nobleman
The Summoner	an official of a church court; corrupt, lewd and offensive
The Pardoner	another unpleasant churchman ; he earns money by selling 'pardons' from Rome, and by letting simple folk see the fake holy relics he carries
The Host	the genial landlord of 'The Tabard', who accompanies them on the pilgrimage, and organises the story-telling
Geoffrey Chaucer	he depicts himself as rather shy and unassuming.

They are later joined by another story teller, **The Canon's Yeoman**, a servant whose tale betrays his master's obsessive interest in alchemy.

A modern pilgrim at Compostela, Spain

68

Pilgrims and pilgrimages

Pilgrimages are journeys made to sacred places, usually as acts of religious devotion. They became increasingly popular during the twelfth and thirteenth centuries, at the time when threats to the Christian world from infidels and heathens from the east reached their height. The passion to defend and reaffirm the power of the Christian church manifested itself in Crusades to the Holy Land, and an upsurge in religious fervour. Shrines were established in many European countries in places of great religious significance. In England, Canterbury Cathedral was the site of the assassination of Archbishop Becket; Walsingham in Norfolk became a holy site of pilgrimage after visions of the Virgin Mary had been seen there. The great cathedral city of Cologne was another centre of pilgrimage, as was Compostela. Further afield, many pilgrims made the long journey to Jerusalem, available for visits from Christian pilgrims after the Emperor Frederick II had negotiated peace with the infidels, and had himself crowned king of the holy city.

Pilgrims, travelling in groups for companionship and safety, would travel to shrines at home and abroad to celebrate their devotion to the church, to seek pardon for their sins, and to ask favours of the saint whose relics were preserved in that place. The traditional image of a pilgrim is of one who travels humbly and simply, dressed in plain clothes, often on foot, carrying a staff. The emblem of a pilgrim is the scallop or cockle shell, worn on cap or hood. This was particularly the symbol of St James, patron saint of military crusaders, and the journey to his shrine in Compostela, in northern Spain, was, and still is, one of the great pilgrim routes across Europe. The shells may originally have been real ones, but were later moulded in lead, as were most other pilgrim badges.

By the time Chaucer decided to use a group of pilgrims as a framework for *The Canterbury Tales*, reasons for pilgrimage had become less exclusively devotional. It was certainly a profitable business for enterprising people, as well as a popular pastime. The tourist industry began to take off. The Venetians offered a regular ferry service carrying travellers to and from the Holy Land. The monks of Cluny, the greatest religious house in France, ran a string of hostels along the entire route between their monastery and Compostela. Travel guides were produced, giving information about accommodation available along the route. One for Compostela contained useful Basque vocabulary, and a description of what to see in the cathedral. Horse traders did a healthy trade in hiring out horses to pilgrims.

There was great competition for popular relics between the religious establishments, which sometimes led to rather obvious forgeries. At least two places, for instance, claimed to possess the head of John the Baptist. Pilgrims began to bring home their own souvenirs, and to house them in their local churches, like the fourteenth century traveller William Wey, who proudly deposited in his Wiltshire village church his maps, a reproduction of St Veronica's handkerchief, which he had rubbed on the pillars of 'the tempyl of Jerusalem', and a large number of stones picked up in sites around the Holy Land. Badges and emblems made of lead were sold at shrines, and eagerly purchased as souvenirs by travellers – the cockle shell for St James, the palm tree from Jericho. At Canterbury it was possible to buy an assortment of badges – an image of the head of the saint, St Thomas riding a horse, a little bell, or a small ampulla [bottle] to hold sacred water. Permission was given from Rome for the local religious houses to obtain a licence to manufacture these.

Some of Chaucer's pilgrims seem to have genuinely devout reasons for visiting Canterbury: the Knight, for instance, has come straight from his military expeditions abroad, fighting for Christendom, and his simple coat is still stained from its contact with his coat of mail. On the other hand, the Wife of Bath, although an enthusiastic pilgrim, hardly seems to be travelling in a spirit of piety or devotion. She lists the places she has visited like a seasoned traveller determined to visit as many tourist attractions as possible. By using a pilgrimage as the frame on which to hang his stories and characterisations, Chaucer was able to point out the way in which attitudes and standards were changing and old values were being lost.

Geoffrey Chaucer

Geoffrey Chaucer

BIOGRAPHICAL NOTES

1340? The actual date of his birth is uncertain, but he was near 60 when he died. His father and grandfather were both vintners – wealthy London merchants, who supplied wines to the king's court.

Chaucer was introduced to court life in his teens. By the age of 16 he was employed in the service of the wife of the king's son, Lionel, later Duke of Clarence.

1359 He fought in France in the army of Edward III. He was captured and imprisoned, but released on payment of his ransom by the duke.

Chaucer was clearly valued by the king and other members of the royal family. In the **1360s** and **1370s** he was sent abroad on diplomatic missions to France, Genoa, Florence and Lombardy.

1360s He married Philippa de Roet, a maid-in-waiting to Edward III's wife, Queen Philippa. Philippa Chaucer's half-sister was Katherine Swynford, third wife of John of Gaunt. The link with this powerful Duke of Lancaster was an important one; the duke was Chaucer's patron and friend, who in later life gave Chaucer a pension of £10 a year.

1368? Chaucer wrote *The Book of the Duchess*, a poem on the death of Duchess Blanche, first wife of John of Gaunt.

1374 The position of Comptroller of Customs for the port of London was given to Chaucer, and in the same year the king granted him a pitcher of wine daily. Other lucrative administrative posts became his later.

1374? Chaucer began his unfinished work *The House of Fame*.

1382? Chaucer wrote *The Parlement of Fowles* – possibly for the marriage of Richard II.

1386 Like the Franklin in *The Canterbury Tales*, Chaucer was appointed 'Knight of the Shire' or parliamentary representative for the county of Kent.

Early 1380s He wrote *Troilus and Criseyde*.

It seems that, in spite of the royal and noble patronage he enjoyed, Chaucer was an extravagant man, and money slipped through his fingers. In **1389** he was appointed Clerk of the King's Works by Richard II, but the position lasted only two years.

Richard later gave him a pension of £20 for life, which Chaucer frequently asked for 'in advance'. Threats of arrest for non-payment of debts were warded off by letters of protection from the crown.

c. 1388 Chaucer probably began to formulate his ideas for *The Canterbury Tales* around this time.

1391 He was appointed deputy forester (an administrative post) in Petherton, Somerset, and may have spent some time there.

| 1399 | Henry IV, son of John of Gaunt, became king, and Chaucer was awarded a new pension of 40 marks (about £26), which allowed him to live his few remaining months in comfort. |
| 1400 | Chaucer died in October, and was buried in Westminster Abbey. |

CHAUCER THE WRITER AND SCHOLAR

Geoffrey Chaucer was actively involved in diplomatic life, moving in court circles, and travelling extensively; he was also an extremely well-read man. His writing shows the influence of classical authors, as well as more recent French and Italian works. The wide range of biblical, classical and contemporary literary references in *The Canterbury Tales* bears witness to his learning, and he confesses to owning 60 books – a very large library in those days. Many of the ideas and themes in the Tales have been adapted from the works of classical and contemporary sources known to Chaucer and to at least some of his audiences.

His earliest works, such as *The Book of the Duchess*, show the influence of courtly and allegorical French love poetry, in particular the *Roman de la Rose*, a dream poem about the psychology of falling in love. The Book of the Duchess is a dream poem in this tradition.

The House of Fame, an unfinished narrative poem, shows influences from both French and Italian poetry. Chaucer admired Dante's works, as well as the writings of two other Italians, Petrarch and Boccaccio, whose works he encountered whilst on diplomatic business in Italy. In fact, Boccaccio's *Decameron*, written forty years or so before *The Canterbury Tales*, employs the linking device (in his case a group of sophisticated men and women, entertaining one another with story-telling in a country retreat, whilst the Black Death rages in Florence) that Chaucer was to use later with far greater subtlety, variety and skill.

In both *Troilus and Criseyde*, his re-telling of the tale of love and betrayal at the time of the Trojan War, and *The Canterbury Tales*, Chaucer shows the debt he owed to classical writers, in particular Ovid and Virgil. He was well acquainted with the Bible (both the Old and New Testaments and the Apocrypha) and he knew something of the writings of theologians respected in the Middle Ages, such as St Jerome and St Augustine. He greatly admired the Roman philosopher Boethius, whose work *De Consolatione Philosophiae* (The Consolation of Philosophy) he translated from its original Latin into English. His writing shows an interest in astronomy and astrology and he wrote *A Treatise on the Astrolabe*, explaining the workings of this astronomical instrument, which he dedicated to 'little Lewis', presumably a young son who died in infancy – we hear nothing of him later.

Background to the Pardoner's Tale

THE FUNCTION OF PARDONERS

The work of a pardoner, an office long since abolished, was bound up with Christian beliefs and teachings on confession. There are three elements or conditions for confession. A penitent must:

- repent his or her sins
- confess them to a priest
- be prepared to carry out the penance or punishment imposed by the priest.

God's absolution of the penitent's guilt can then be pronounced by the priest. Any failure in these three conditions on the part of the penitent renders the absolution null and void.

The state of the soul is important to the Christian preparing for the next life. Though most people are weak and sinful, it was difficult to think that many people were so wicked that their souls would end up in the fires of hell; and similarly, though some people are saintlike, it was difficult to think of large numbers of souls gaining entry to heaven immediately upon death. Most souls would remain for some time in purgatory, being cleansed of their sins and made fit for heaven. The earthly penances given at confession would assist them in this, as could the prayers of those left behind on earth. This remission of purgatory was known as an indulgence.

A medieval representation of the mouth of hell

Penances in the middle ages were very severe, and over many centuries another approach was established in which money could be paid as a substitute, rather like paying a fine instead of going to prison. Both are unwelcome to wrong-doers, but payment is perhaps less unattractive. The money could then be used by the church for its various religious and charitable purposes.

The beliefs and motives are subtle, and illiterate penitents might see this as something simpler, like a market transaction. Others, such as Chaucer's Pardoner, might be tempted to exploit the system for their own purposes: something is for sale, and if you can convince people who want it that you have the right and power to provide it, the whole thing becomes a profitable racket. The worst part of such a racket is that it involves trading upon people's beliefs and fears. Perhaps part of the Host's anger at the end of the Pardoner's Tale is due to his disgust at the electrifyingly honest way the Pardoner has explained the tricks of his trade to the pilgrims.

Chaucer's pilgrims would know that the Pardoner is not a clergyman. He has no power to pronounce absolution for people's sins, and he has no right to preach, this being a function reserved for priests. The source of his licence to practice as a Pardoner is glossed over, and, given the dishonesty he proclaims throughout his Prologue and Tale, it is unlikely to be authentic. He makes his own pronouncement on the authenticity of his relics.

MEDIEVAL SERMONS

In a largely illiterate age, people could learn their religion only in their own local church. They could watch and listen to the ritual and ceremony of the mass and they were supposed to have received instruction on its meaning. They could look at the often rather unskilled pictures of biblical scenes painted upon the walls, a few of which are still to be seen. They had prayer and the sacraments. They had the example of their priest (and were fortunate if he were someone like Chaucer's Parson) and other saintly people (like the Plowman); and they had sermons.

Preaching was a highly developed technique in the middle ages, and like many things in those days, it had an agreed structure, widely disseminated in manuals of instruction, which no doubt formed an important part of a priest's training.

There were six parts to the sermon:
- the statement of the theme, usually a biblical text – *Radix malorum est cupiditas* in this case
- an introduction
- an illustrative story as an example relevant to people's lives
- the development – an examination and explanation of the text
- a discussion of the application of the text to people's lives
- a conclusion and blessing.

This was backed up by smaller examples drawn from the scriptures or other authoritative writers, fitted in at suitable moments throughout the sermon. It is possible, with some thought, to find all these stages in the Pardoner's Prologue and Tale.

The manuals also recommend many stylistic devices to hold the congregation's attention, and to make the content of the sermon more memorable. Repetition was important, as nothing was written, and the sermon could only be significant if people remembered something of it. The Pardoner sometimes uses what was technically known as exclamation in order to underline his point, as when he says in lines 609-13:

> O cursed sinne of alle cursednesse!
> O traitours homicide, O wikkednesse!
> O glotonye, luxurie, and hasardrye!
> Thou blasphemour of Crist with vilenye
> And othes grete, of usage and of pride!

The action of preaching was and is intended to bring the people closer to Christ. The preacher is not giving his own self-generated thoughts but he is passing on the word of God; he is a kind of channel rather than a performer, and should not intrude himself, or hope for applause or his own glorification. The Pardoner makes it clear at several points that he thoroughly enjoys his powers of persuasion, and that he is very conscious of his technique. Yet it is possible to see in his sermon a marvellous example of the art delivered with the worst of motives and with the utmost contempt for his congregation. He is playing with them, for amusement as well as for gain, and his acquaintance with the sins he is condemning makes his success all the more vivid for Chaucer's readers, especially at those moments when the sermon is plain funny, or when he is blasphemous while condemning blasphemy.

75

SIN IN THE PARDONER'S TALE

Christianity sees sin as wounding to God. The three rioters described by Chaucer are given over to a variety of sins that lead on, one from another, until the men die. They start with gluttony, much discussed by the Pardoner, they gamble, they insult an old man, they blaspheme, they lie, they cheat, and they kill.

There is a sense in which the work sees all sins as the same sin:
- in the obvious sense that they are all wounding to God
- in the sense that one sin leads to another
- in the sense that all sins are a form of blasphemy – which may be defined as insulting and attacking God. The rioters, for instance, decide to find and kill Death. In Christian belief this is something that can only be the work of God, and to attempt to replace God in this way is a profound sin.

Blasphemy sums up sin in the work. Time after time the rioters, or the Pardoner himself, or the Host on occasion, break out with gratuitous oaths, taking the name of God in vain. The effect of all this is seen as subjecting Christ to re-crucifixion – the Tale makes this clear in lines 186-190:

> Hir othes been so grete and so dampnable
> That it is grisly for to heere hem swere.
> Oure blissed Lordes body they totere –
> Hem thoughte that Jewes rente him noght ynough;
> And ech of hem at otheres sinne lough.

The story of the crucifixion, with all its appalling physical and mental anguish, would have been as familiar to Chaucer's pilgrims as the details of their own existence. Some of them would also have been able to see metaphorical re-crucifixion in the words and actions of the Prologue and Tale, and their presence on a pilgrimage would perhaps have made them more than usually sensitive to this level of meaning.

The Pardoner seems unmoved by this. Is he foolish, to lay open his way of life like this? He has thought about it – he asked for time (and a drink) in order to prepare the right tale – yet he is angry and mortified when the Host excoriates him at the end. Where does he stand in relation to sin? If we are even to approach an answer to this question we have to look at some of his statements, particularly when he says in lines 141-5:

> Thus kan I preche again that same vice
> Which that I use, and that is avarice.
> But though myself be gilty in that sinne,
> Yet can I maken oother folk to twynne
> From avarice, and soore to repente.

Here he is touching on a large theological debate of the time: can an evil man preach the truth? Can he even know the truth? One school of thought held that knowledge is love, and therefore an evil person can effectively know nothing. Another view was that the intellect and the will were different, and as knowledge was a matter of the intellect, and love was a matter of will, it was possible for a working intellect to know the truth while a defective will made the same person blind to love.

The Pardoner, not surprisingly, argues for the second point of view. He would hold that if he says words, thinking them to be untrue but knowing that his hearers will think them true and beneficial, and he makes a good living from it, where is the sin?

He says of his relics 'Relikes been they, as wenen they echoon' (line 63). In other words they are holy relics, with all their powers and effects, if people think they are. The Pardoner thinks they are animal bones, but they do him a power of good financially. It is a slippery world in which he lives, and if he can spin with words a web of apparent meaning that is satisfactory to his audience, why should he not? This is perhaps why he is so open with everybody about what he does, and why, having declared his motives and revealed his practices, he still tries to sell his pardons and relics to the pilgrims at the conclusion of his tale.

This suggests a way of looking at the world very far removed from the solid structures of medieval beliefs. A world without meaning is not a Christian world; it is a world without anything except a casual series of fortuitous events which can be manipulated by some people for their own advantage. It is certainly a world without God, because it is a world containing no reality outside any individual's mind. Indeed, it would be difficult to call it a 'world' in the sense of a purposeful or ordered universe; it is just a chaos which some individuals prefer not to see as a chaos.

Chaucer's self-examination as a poet

It is possible to see further significance in this for Chaucer as a word-spinner – that is, as a poet. If people can be persuaded, by hearing or reading words, to see something meaningful to them individually, are the words of the poet any more reliable than the Pardoner's words? Where is their meaning? In the poet's mind or in the listeners' responses? Or just in the words themselves, as meaning whatever people think them to mean?

Chaucer constantly undercuts himself in *The Canterbury Tales*, most obviously at those points when he presents himself as a character within his work, and gives that character an amiable, bumbling foolishness. By doing so, he seems to be raising not only the question of meaning but also the question of what poetry is and what language is.

This is not to suggest that Chaucer is a kind of poetic Pardoner, exploiting the credulity of his readers. Whatever is going on in *The Canterbury Tales*, there are meanings being communicated by his poem that we can all agree on; it is reasonable to think that these are what Chaucer intended, and that Chaucer, unlike his creation, the Pardoner, thought words were more than just a means of persuading and exploiting people.

The role of the church

SOCIETY AND THE CHURCH

The church exerted its influence over all aspects of fourteenth century society life.

- Everyone was expected to attend mass and other services, to make regular confessions and to give offerings to the church.
- Such hospitals and schools as existed were run by monasteries, who also offered hospitality to travellers.
- Almost the only drama or colour in people's lives came from the ritual of the mass, from church music and from the paintings of biblical scenes on the walls of their churches. They would have enjoyed well-rehearsed and well-delivered sermons such as the one we hear given by the Pardoner. The travelling Friars belonged to orders dedicated to bringing Christ's message to remote places, and it would have been surprising if their relatively few sermons, preached constantly to new congregations, did not become polished performances.
- Monastic orders had been gathering vast estates over many centuries, usually left to them by pious landowners, and they employed many lay people to help run them. The monks themselves were usually drawn from the middle class, and comprised less than half the population of the monasteries in the fourteenth century. In the great cathedral towns such as York and Canterbury, and in the areas around the largest and richest monasteries, the church had considerable control over the population, not just spiritually, but over wages as employers, housing as landlords, and food supplies as landowners. This was despite a growing and thriving merchant class in such cities.
- The church had real political power. Well into the fourteenth century the position of Chancellor, treasurer of the realm, was usually held by a churchman – whose allegiance was not just to his king but also to the Pope. St Thomas of Canterbury was a cleric whose dilemma in this post led to his murder in 1170.
- Church courts of law had considerable privileges. The clergy could not be tried and sentenced in the ordinary law courts, whatever their crime, and the church courts gave them protection not available to others, including the right of appeal to the Pope.

GROWING DISCONTENT

It was inconceivable that such a dominant institution should escape criticism. There was a long tradition of literary satire, already two centuries old by Chaucer's time, and well-established among the French poets he read and admired. Some of Chaucer's own satirical and humorous criticisms of the clerical pilgrims can be seen as part of this literary tradition, which focused largely on two areas of discontent: complaints about church wealth, and complaints about the behaviour of churchmen.

- The Commons declared that one-third of the country's wealth lay in the hands of the church. Even the travelling orders of Friars (originally founded in reaction to the laxity and wealth of the church) had become property-owning institutions, often as rich and as worldly as the others.

- Priests urged congregations to lead sober and virtuous lives, but some provided poor examples themselves. Some became parish priests for the revenue they could obtain, then 'farmed out' the parish work for a pittance to substitutes. Stories about bad behaviour in monasteries and nunneries were common and widely enjoyed. Original monastic standards of poverty, chastity and sober godliness were always in danger of neglect, and over the centuries many new orders had been founded with the intention of re-asserting these ideals.

LOSS OF INFLUENCE

In the fourteenth century the church began to lose some of its great influence.

- John Wyclif, a great scholar and philosopher at Oxford University, suggested powerful theological reasons why the church should own no property. He believed that academic centres should be free from undue church influence. His followers, known as Lollards, travelled the country preaching an evangelical religion drawn from the Bible, newly translated into English.
- The fourteenth century was a time of growth in towns, with their industry and trade. People became more prosperous and settled. In this atmosphere, criticism of the church became more vocal and widespread.
- Learning from the techniques that had made the monasteries so wealthy, secular landowners began to mange their own estates more efficiently.
- More people were learning to read and write by going to school, and many of the schools were set up outside church control. For instance, in 1382 the wealthy and successful William of Wykeham founded a comprehensive school at Winchester, with scholarships to support children as poor as he had been, on the principle that it is 'manners' (i.e. behaviour, not birth) that 'makyth man'.
- The powerful monasteries in the south east of England were ferociously attacked during the Peasants' Revolt of 1381. The rebel leader, Wat Tyler, beheaded the Archbishop of Canterbury on Tower Hill.

While it would be wrong, therefore, to read Chaucer's picture of the church in *The Canterbury Tales* as an even-handed or objective description, there is no doubt that his unforgettable caricatures – the hypocritical Friar, the greedy Monk – would have been recognised and enjoyed by the successful nobles and self-confident townsmen who formed his audience. That type of churchman belonged to an old economic and social order, under general attack in the years when Chaucer was writing, and the old order's grip was perhaps further loosened by *The Canterbury Tales*.

Themes in the Pardoner's Prologue and Tale

1 CHAUCER'S STYLE

a) What methods does he use to vary the style in keeping with his presentation of the character of the Pardoner?

b) How, and how effectively, does the writer create for the reader an idea of medieval life and times?

c) Is he funny? subtle? scathing? lively? learned? descriptive? scholarly? Find examples from the text to illustrate the points you make.

d) Chaucer was extremely widely read. How far does his own scholarship and literary knowledge add to what he says?

e) Do you think the Pardoner's Prologue and Tale would be more effective read silently or aloud?

2 TALE AND TELLER

a) Would you say this Tale is appropriate for the teller?

b) Write a brief summary of the Tale. Comment on its qualities as a story, for example, structure, pace, variation, colloquial language, conversation.

c) How are such things as avarice, hypocrisy, blasphemy, justice handled in both the Prologue and the Tale?

d) Which is the Pardoner's Tale – the tale of the three rioters and death, his sermon, or his prologue?

3 CHAUCER AND THE FOURTEENTH CENTURY

a) What do we learn about religion and attitudes to it?

b) How much power and authority did pardoners really have?

c) Does Chaucer create a really believable character here, or a stereotype? And can we, today, identify with either?

4 IRONY

a) Is the Pardoner's sermon effective? Could he save others but not himself?

b) The rioters' search for Death is successful. Where do they find it?

c) Why should the Pardoner say that the Host is the one who is 'moost envoluped in sinne'?

Glossary of frequently-used words

agoon	past	oon	one
algate	all the same	othes	oaths
annexed	linked	povre	poor
anoon	immediately	smale	small
ay	always	sondry	various
bitwixen	between	swoote	sweet
boghte	bought	taak kep	take heed
devise	describe	toun	town
eek	also	tweye	two
fond	found	verray	true, real, exact
forby	past	wenen	believe, suppose
gan	began	weneth	thinks
hente	seize	woodnesse	madness
hool	whole	yeven	given
it is no drede	there	yholde	considered is no doubt
koude	knew how to	yshriven	absolved
nyste	did not know		